the weekly poem

the weekly poem

52 exercises in closed & open forms

It's such a blessed relief to have some little formal problem to work out,
so you don't have to think about the earthshaking importance of what
you are going to say.

—Howard Nemerov

Limitation makes for power . . .

—Richard Wilbur

Jordie Albiston

PUNCHER & WATTMANN

Contents

Introduction

Exercises are essential to any art form. Whether it is life drawing for the artist, barre work for the dancer, or scales and arpeggios for the musician, exercises provide a foundation upon which competence and eventual proficiency may be built. Exercises keep one nimble and alert. They challenge parameters while increasing and maintaining musculature. They teach discipline, focus and new ways of seeing. While inspiration and natural ability may come as gifts, technical skill is a thing attained only by endeavour and the act of doing.

All art requires structure. But how does one know which organisational techniques will best convey the meaning, energy and spirit of the poem one wants to write? Ideally, such decision-making occurs instinctively, without too much outside thought. However, sometimes a poem seems intractable and will not give itself easily to the page. While not every poet seeks to be a sonneteer or master of haiku, there is much to be gained from writing in a variety of forms. A simple idea gleaned from such practice—repeating a line, introducing a syllable count, breaking a poem into sub-titled sections—may impart the precise counter to an otherwise unresolved poem.

While this book has been designed predominantly with teachers and students in mind, it will serve any poet—at any stage—wanting to stimulate their discipline. Its exercises are formatted in shorthand, one to a page. Rather than relying on extended prose commentaries, tasks are explained in point form, allowing the reader a concise overview of what and how at a glance. Each exercise is accompanied by a reading list of relevant sample poems; while these poems range across time, culture and place, Australian poetry is the principal focus. Sometimes a sample poem will relate to the task in terms of form: sometimes subject or theme. A selection of poems per exercise is printed in full. All listed poems are readily accessible through contemporary anthologies, individual collections or the internet, with a full bibliography supplied at the back.

The Weekly Poem aims to impart an insight into the world of formal and informal poetics— both traditional and modern—by which solutions to problems may be found. Its exercises are relevant to poets endeavouring to expand their capacity to understand, and thereby exploit, their own writing process. Writing poetry can provide an outlet for the creative self, a method for wresting order from chaos, an access to the silent interior. Writing poetry can be a source of witness, of wonder, of wellbeing. Writing poetry can be pure pleasure, and it is hoped that this book offers its own source of enjoyment—week to week—as much as it seeks to instruct.

Acrostic

THEME:	open
FORM:	vertical monochord
RHYME SCHEME:	none
METRE:	none
LINE LENGTH:	variable
POEM LENGTH:	maximum one page

— see MONOCHORD

BACKGROUND:
— 'acrostic' from Greek (at the tip of the verse)
— ancient form (*Book of Lamentations*, Babylonian texts c. 1000BC, Jesus 'fish')
— popular during Renaissance as device to conceal message

FORM:
— left-hand initials spell out name/title/phrase/sentence vertically
— medial letters (through middle) = mesostich
— final letters = telestich
— both initials & finals = double acrostic
— initials, medials & finals = triple acrostic
— acrostic can read top to bottom, bottom to top, or as anagram (concealment)
— acrostic may also be dispersed throughout poem > first letter of each *sentence* (rather than first letter of each *line*)

TASK:
— select last two or three words from a monochord
   "later, someone said they'd seen a *bird on fire*"
   "the first thing he heard was *drums in the sky*"
   "there is no cure for *the forgotten heart*"
— arrange words vertically down left-hand margin
— construct poem with lines beginning with these letters
— employ stanza break between words
— use upper-case for first letter each line (emphasise acrostic)
— enjambment encouraged
— attempt to extricate/develop meaning from selected phrase

READING:
— Emily Mary Barton 'Acrostic on New South Wales the Fairies' Scheme' *www.poetrylibrary.edu.au*
— Lewis Carroll 'Life is But a Dream' *The Annotated Alice*
— Billy Collins 'The Names' (dispersed alphabetic acrostic) *Poets Laureate Anthology*
— Gwen Harwood 'Eloisa to Abelard', 'Abelard to Eloisa' *Mappings of the Plane*
— Anita Heiss 'Sorry' *Motherlode*
— John Keats 'Acrostic' *John Keats: The Complete Poems*
— John Tranter 'Girl in Water' (double acrostic) *www.poetrylibrary.edu.au*

Eloisa to Abelard
—Gwen Harwood

Solace and hope depart. God's finger traces
on fields of frozen darkness: You shall find
loss, absence, nothing. Walking on the wind
Our Lord speaks to a crowd of foolish faces,

no face that is not mine, while filtering through
gaps, honeycombs of memory you seem
but the faint ghost of a remembered dream.
Unveiled by pain, I bleed. My wound is you.

Lost in the well of space, my spirit hears
'Lucis creator optime. . .' The choir
entreats God, out of tune. I join my voice
to theirs. Nightfall's immense. I taste my tears.
I reap the harvest of my own desire.
No heart escapes the torment of its choice.

Abelard to Eloisa
—Gwen Harwood

Far above memory's landscape let the fears
unlatched from thundering valleys of your mind
carry their lightning. Stare the sun up. Find
kinetic heat to scorch your mist of tears.

All that your vision limned by night appears
loose in dismembering air: think yourself blind.
Louder than death in headlines the unkind
elements hawk my passion: stop your ears.

Deny me now. Be Doubting Thomas. Thrust
into my side the finger of your grief.
Tell me I am an apparition frayed
out of the tattered winding-sheet of lust.
Recall no ghost of love. Let no belief
summon me, fleshed and bleeding, from the shade.

Anthem

THEME:	Australia
FORM:	quintains
RHYME SCHEME:	ababB/cdcdB/efefB
METRE:	none
STRUCTURE:	decasyllabic
POEM LENGTH:	3 stanzas

— see SYLLABIC POEM

TASK:
— compose a national anthem in 5-line stanzas, exactly 10 syllables per line
— anthem may be positive or negative but must evoke a sense of truth
— explore what Australia may represent within a specific context:
  indigenous
  immigrant
  convict
  sport/arts
  world view
  religion
  physical environment/s
— choose a symbol to represent 'your' Australia:
  boomerang
  suitcase
  ball & chain
  football
  upside-down map
  flora/fauna
— develop & sustain symbolism throughout poem
— utilise language effectively
  demotic idiom/colloquialisms
  broken English
  hymn
  team/club song
  propaganda
  travel brochure
  advertising jingle
— repeat refrain as last line of each stanza ('B')
— attempt a 'singable' poem . . .

READING:
— Gary Catalano 'Australia' *Australian Poetry Since 1788*
— Toby Davidson 'Skyshow' *Beast Language*
— Allen Ginsberg 'America' *Howl, Kaddish and Other Poems*
— Peter Goldsworthy 'Australia' *Macquarie PEN Anthology*
— A.D. Hope 'Australia' *P&W Anthology of Australian Poetry*
— Dorothea Mackellar 'My Country' *P&W Anthology of Australian Poetry*
— Ania Walwicz 'Australia' *P&W Anthology of Australian Poetry*
— Judith Wright 'Australia 1970' *P&W Anthology of Australian Poetry*

My Country
—Dorothea Mackellar

The love of field and coppice
　　　Of green and shaded lanes,
Of ordered woods and gardens
　　　Is running in your veins.
Strong love of grey-blue distance
　　　Brown streams and soft, dim skies—
I know but cannot share it,
　　　My love is otherwise.

I love a sunburnt country,
　　　A land of sweeping plains,
Of ragged mountain ranges,
　　　Of droughts and flooding rains.
I love her far horizons,
　　　I love her jewel-sea,
Her beauty and her terror—
　　　The wide brown land for me!

The stark white ring-barked forests,
　　　All tragic to the moon,
The sapphire-misted mountains,
　　　The hot gold hush of noon.
Green tangle of the brushes,
　　　Where lithe lianas coil,
And orchids deck the tree tops
　　　And ferns the warm dark soil.

Core of my heart, my country!
　　　Her pitiless blue sky,
When sick at heart, around us,
　　　We see the cattle die—
But then the grey clouds gather,
　　　And we can bless again
The drumming of an army,
　　　The steady, soaking rain.

Core of my heart, my country!
　　　Land of the Rainbow Gold,
For flood and fire and famine,
　　　She pays us back three-fold.
Over the thirsty paddocks,
　　　Watch, after many days,
The filmy veil of greenness
　　　That thickens as we gaze . . .

An opal-hearted country,
　　　A wilful, lavish land—
All you who have not loved her,

You will not understand—
Though earth holds many splendours,
　　　Wherever I may die,
I know to what brown country
　　　My homing thoughts will fly.

Australia
—Ania Walwicz

You big ugly. You too empty. You desert with your nothing nothing nothing. You scorched suntanned. Old too quickly. Acres of suburbs watching the telly. You bore me. Freckle silly children. You nothing much. With your big sea. Beach beach beach. I've seen enough already. You dumb dirty city with bar stools. You're ugly. You silly shoppingtown. You copy. You too far everywhere. You laugh at me. When I came this woman gave me a box of biscuits. You try to be friendly but you're not very friendly. You never ask me to your house. You insult me. You don't know how to be with me. Road road tree tree. I came from crowded and many. I came from rich. You have nothing to offer. You're poor and spread thin. You big. So what. I'm small. It's what's in. You silent on Sunday. Nobody on your streets. You dead at night. You go to sleep too early. You don't excite me. You scare me with your hopeless. Asleep when you walk. Too hot to think. You big awful. You don't match me. You burnt out. You too big sky. You make me a dot in the nowhere. You laugh with your big healthy. You want everyone to be the same. You're dumb. You do like anybody else. You engaged Doreen. You big cow. You average average. Cold day at school playing around at lunchtime. Running around for nothing. You never accept me. For your own. You always ask me where I'm from. You always ask me. You tell me I look strange. Different. You don't adopt me. You laugh at the way I speak. You think you're better than me. You don't like me. You don't have any interest in another country. Idiot centre of your own self. You think the rest of the world walks around without shoes or electric light. You don't go anywhere. You stay at home. You like one another. You go crazy on Saturday night. You get drunk. You don't like me and you don't like women. You put your arm around men in bars. You're rough. I can't speak to you. You burly burly. You're just silly to me. You big man. Poor with all your money. You ugly furniture. You ugly house. Relaxed in your summer stupor. All year. Never fully awake. Dull at school. Wait for other people to tell you what to do. Follow the leader. Can't imagine. Work horse. Thick legs. You go to work in the morning. You shiver on a tram.

Australia
—Peter Goldsworthy

Our earthen dish is seven parts water,
one part china, and a tiny bit japanned.
Its spread of foods is well-presented:
ice sculptures at both poles, and licking-salt
elsewhere. Give me a lever large enough—
a cosmic fork or skewer—and I would take it
to a table: its sherbet fizz of surf,
the creamy ice-cones of its toothy alps,
the spice of islands dotted here and there
like cloves jammed in an onion. Turning
this common dish as slowly as a day, I'd taste
the sweet-and-sour river deltas, the swamps
about its world wide waist, all of which
smell fishy. As do many maps of Tasmania,
most of them in other places: forest fuzz
itchy with green pubic life. Lastly comes
our smaller plate, single and tectonic:
our turf, or lack of it, our baked and gritty
crust, lightly watered, sifter dusted,
and sarcastic with odd hints of eucalypt.
Its thousand mile creek tastes too salty,
its muddy waters barely moving, but still
moving enough to stir a homesick heart.

Skyshow
—Toby Davidson

Fireworks now and fire worked then, as long as it sparkles
we'll claim Bethlehem. Bottled sparkle, served on buildings
rains forty stories down on mounted police as they baton-charge
youths, including at least three Darrens I saw tearing each other
to *garn fuggun gah-un* as their girlfriends screamed *Darren, Darren*
and more joined in cos it's a free country of battlers you can't stop
the music feeling no pain punching headfuls of shirt with a smoke
in one hand pissing green and gold darkness from an old semi-naked
twist top shrapnel wound . . . I'll never forget the bloke who told his
opponent *Ah pull yer pants up, mate* before socking him straight
in the chops. To summarise: we are a noble people, unable to bear
ourselves without booze, if we can't blow things up we just fight
for the hell of it, our national day is a crucible of destruction,
and I want to go home, I just want to go home, but this is where I live.

Ballad

THEME:	suburbia
FORM:	cross-rhyming quatrains
RHYME SCHEME:	abab *or* abcb
METRE:	iambic tetrameter/iambic trimeter
POEM LENGTH:	8 quatrains
TENSE:	past
TONE:	demotic/colloquial

—   see METRICAL POEM

BACKGROUND:
— 'ballad' from Italian *ballare* (to dance) > ballet/ball
— origins in folk/popular song > C14th
— early connections to dance/ritual
— found in every country/language
— short narrative poem > tells a story
— traditionally concerned with public events/current affairs/local concerns
— balladeer's voice distinct/human
— form still in use > team songs/country & western/rap

FORM:
— 4-line stanzas
— 1st & 3rd lines in iambic tetrameter (4 beats)
  2nd & 4th lines in iambic trimeter (3 beats) > or tetrameter with 'silent' 4th beat
— characterised by regional vernacular/dialogue > plain language
— vivid imagery to impel telling of tale > brief/dramatic scenes

TASK:
— construct a poem in 4-line stanzas
— utilise story & metre as devices to push poem forward
— enjoy rhythmic lilt of form > allow poem to sing/swing along

READING:
— anonymous 'The Wife of Usher's Well' *Norton Anthology of Poetry*
— John Betjeman 'Death in Leamington' *Norton Anthology of Poetry*
— Rodney Hall 'Mrs Macintosh' *Penguin Anthology of Australian Poetry*
— Gwen Harwood 'Suburban Sonnet' *Penguin Anthology of Australian Poetry*
— Coral Hull 'Liverpool' *P&W Anthology of Australian Poetry*
— Mike Ladd 'Junior Football' *Penguin Anthology of Australian Poetry*
— Les Murray 'The Ballad Trap' *Collected Poems*
— Oodgeroo Noonuccal 'Ballad of the Totems' *P&W Anthology of Australian Poetry*
— Alan Wearne 'Knox City: a Ballad' *Australian Poetry Since 1788*

The Wife of Usher's Well
—anonymous

THERE lived a wife at Usher's Well,
  And a wealthy wife was she;
She had three stout and stalwart sons,
  And sent them o'er the sea.

They hadna been a week from her,
  A week but barely ane,
When word came to the carline wife
  That her three sons were gane.

They hadna been a week from her,
  A week but barely three,
When word came to the carline wife
  That her sons she'd never see.

'I wish the wind may never cease.
  Nor fashes in the flood,
Till my three sons come hame to me,
  In earthly flesh and blood!'

It fell about the Martinmas,
  When nights are lang and mirk,
The carline wife's three sons came hame,
  And their hats were o' the birk.

It neither grew in syke nor ditch,
  Nor yet in ony sheugh;
But at the gates o' Paradise
  That birk grew fair eneugh.

'Blow up the fire, my maidens!
  Bring water from the well!
For a' my house shall feast this night,
  Since my three sons are well.'

And she has made to them a bed,
  She 's made it large and wide;
And she 's ta'en her mantle her about,
  Sat down at the bedside.

Up then crew the red, red cock,
  And up and crew the gray;
The eldest to the youngest said.
  ''Tis time we were away.'

The cock he hadna craw'd but once,
  And clapp'd his wings at a',
When the youngest to the eldest said,
  'Brother, we must awa'.

The cock doth craw, the day doth daw,
  The channerin' worm doth chide;
Gin we be miss'd out o' our place,
  A sair pain we maun bide.'

'Lie still, lie still but a little wee while,
  Lie still but if we may;
Gin my mother should miss us when she wakes,
  She'll go mad ere it be day.'

'Fare ye weel, my mother dear!
  Fareweel to barn and byre!
And fare ye weel, the bonny lass
  That kindles my mother's fire!'

Ballad of the Totems
—Oodgeroo Noonuccal

My father was Noonuccal man and kept old tribal way,
His totem was the Carpet Snake, whom none must ever slay;
But mother was of Peewee clan, and loudly she expressed
The daring view that carpet snakes were nothing but a pest.

Now one lived right inside with us in full immunity,
For no one dared to interfere with father's stern decree:
A mighty fellow ten feet long, and as we lay in bed
We kids could watch him round a beam not far above our head.

Only the dog was scared of him, we'd hear its whines and growls,
But mother fiercely hated him because he took her fowls.
You should have heard her diatribes that flowed in angry torrents
With words you never see in print, except in D. H. Lawrence.

'I kill that robber,' she would scream, fierce as a spotted cat;
'You see that bulge inside of him? My speckly hen make that!'
But father's loud and strict command made even mother quake;
I think he'd sooner kill a man than kill a carpet snake.

That reptile was a greedy-guts, and as each bulge digested
He'd come down on the hunt at night as appetite suggested.
We heard his stealthy slithering sound across the earthen floor,
While the dog gave a startled yelp and bolted out the door.

Then over in the chicken-yard hysterical fowls gave tongue,
Loud frantic squawks accompanied by the barking of the mung,
Until at last the racket passed, and then to solve the riddle,
Next morning he was back up there with a new bulge in his middle.

When father died we wailed and cried, our grief was deep and sore,
And strange to say from that sad day the snake was seen no more.
The wise old men explained to us: 'It was his tribal brother,
And that is why it done a guy'—but some looked hard at mother.

She seemed to have a secret smile, her eyes were smug and wary,
She looked as innocent as the cat that ate the pet canary.
We never knew, but anyhow (to end this tragic rhyme)
I think we all had snake for tea one day about that time.

The Ballad Trap
—Les Murray

In the hanging gorges
the daring compact wears thin,
picking meat from small skeletons,
counting damp notes in a tin,

the rifle birds ringing at noon
in the steep woods,
hard-riding boys dazed at the brink
of their attitudes,

the youngest wheedling for songs,
his back to the night,
dark mountains the very English
for souring delight:

Remember the Escort? Remember
lamps long ago
and manhood filched from the horse police
and a name from Cobb and Co.

Their metre hobbled, the horses
hump their dark life,
longing for marriage, the tall man
sharpens his knife—

Yes, let us sing! cries the Captain
while we have breath.
Better, God knows, than this thinking.
The ballad ends with their death.

Ballade

THEME:	old age
FORM:	3 octaves & 4-line envoi
RHYME SCHEME:	ababbcbC/ababbcbC/ababbcbC/bcbC
SYLLABLES:	8 *or* 10 per line (optional)
METRE:	none
POEM LENGTH:	28 lines

—   see SYLLABIC POEM

BACKGROUND:
—   dominant C14th/C15th French form (Eustache Deschamps/Francois Villon)
—   imitated in English by Chaucer/Gower (decasyllabic > 10 syllables per line)

FORM:
—   fixed/closed form
—   3 x 8-line stanzas rhyming ababbcbC
—   stanzas traditionally consist of octosyllables (8)
—   final 'C' is repetition of entire line (ie: refrain occurs 4 times)
—   envoi (coda) rhyming bcbC
—   envoi frequently addressed to a 'prince' > medieval literary competition . . .
         "Prince" generally first word of envoi
—   here "Prince" may be substituted with:
         Princes
         Princess/es
         King/s
         Queen/s
—   see Gwen Harwood's poem for use of "king"

TASK:
—   write a ballade exploring/lamenting/commemorating old age
—   may be personal or universal
—   attempt to adhere to *all* the rules

READING:
—   G.K. Chesterton 'A Ballade of Suicide' *www.chesterton.org*
—   Jamie Grant 'Ballade of Present Enchantment' *www.poetrylibrary.edu.au*
—   Robert Gray 'In Departing Light' *Coast Road*
—   Gwen Harwood 'Father and Child: Nightfall' *Mappings of the Plane*
—   James McAuley 'Ballade of Lost Phrases' *www.poetrylibrary.edu.au*
—   Dorothy Parker 'Ballade of Unfortunate Mammals' *www.poemhunter.com*
—   Marie E.J. Pitt "Ballade of Bitter Memories' *www.poetrylibrary.edu.au*
—   Francis Webb 'The Old Women' *P&W Anthology of Australian Poetry*

Ballade of Lost Phrases
—James McAuley

In what museum now abide
The pamphlets that we read of yore;
Where are the orators that cried
"We will not fight a bosses' war,"
"The system's not worth fighting for,"
"To Hell with the Jingo profiteer,"
"The Empire's rotten to the core,"
—Where are the phrases of yesteryear?

No longer can it be denied,
The Left Book Club's become a bore;
We're social patriots double-dyed,
And social fascists too, what's more.
We tolerate Sir Samuel Hoare!
Churchill now delights the ear,
And Beaverbrook is to the fore.
—Where are the phrases of yesteryear?

The Party Line from side to side
Zig-zagged till our eyes were sore;
Can it be the Marxists—lied?
Peace to the shades of *Inprecorr*!
The left wing's moulting on our shore:
It will not fly again, I fear.
Freedom has become a whore.
—Where are the phrases of yesteryear?

Envoi

Comrades, we argued, fought and swore:
We might as well have stuck to beer.
The Japanese are in Johore
—Where are the phrases of yesteryear?

Ballade of Unfortunate Mammals
—Dorothy Parker

Love is sharper than stones or sticks;
Lone as the sea, and deeper blue;
Loud in the night as a clock that ticks;
Longer-lived than the Wandering Jew.
Show me a love was done and through,
Tell me a kiss escaped its debt!
Son, to your death you'll pay your due—
Women and elephants never forget.

Ever a man, alas, would mix,
Ever a man, heigh-ho, must woo;
So he's left in the world-old fix,
Thus is furthered the sale of rue.
Son, your chances are thin and few—
Won't you ponder, before you're set?
Shoot if you must, but hold in view
Women and elephants never forget.

Down from Caesar past Joynson-Hicks
Echoes the warning, ever new:
Though they're trained to amusing tricks,
Gentler, they, than the pigeon's coo,
Careful, son, of the curs'ed two—
Either one is a dangerous pet;
Natural history proves it true—
Women and elephants never forget.

L'ENVOI

Prince, a precept I'd leave for you,
Coined in Eden, existing yet:
Skirt the parlor, and shun the zoo—
Women and elephants never forget.

Blank Verse

THEME:	a swim or dive
FORM:	block
METRE:	iambic pentameter
RHYME SCHEME:	none
POEM LENGTH:	maximum 24 lines

—   see METRICAL POEM

BACKGROUND:
—   from Italian *verse sciolti da rima* (verse free from rhyme)
—   roots in classical/epic poetry > Renaissance
—   appears in English C16th (Henry Howard > translated *The Aeneid*)
—   rigorously developed by Christopher Marlowe/Shakespeare (plays)/John Milton

FORM:
—   consists of iambic 5-beat lines
—   lack of rhyme allows for enjambment/natural speech rhythms
—   often comprises long sentences > complex description/thought

TASK:
—   compose a sustained piece of poetic description
—   employ prolonged sentences to evoke progression of idea > one long stanza
—   tell story of swim/dive > before/during/after

READING:
—   Catherine Bateson 'Learning to Swim' *P&W Anthology of Australian Poetry*
—   Bruce Dawe 'Reverie of a Swimmer' *Sometimes Gladness*
—   Stephen Edgar 'The Immortals' *Other Summers*
—   Paul Hetherington 'Early Ambition' *Six Different Windows*
—   Barry Hill 'A Long Swim' *Penguin Anthology of Australian Poetry*
—   L.K. Holt 'Noon Swim' *Man Wolf Man*
—   Peter Minter 'Afternoon Swim, 22/11/91' *www.poetrylibrary.edu.au*
—   Adrienne Rich 'Diving Into the Wreck' *Norton Anthology of Poetry*
—   Tom Shapcott 'Skin Diver' *www.poetrylibrary.edu.au*
—   R.A. Simpson 'Diver' *Penguin Anthology of Australian Poetry*
—   William Wordsworth '*The Prelude*' *Works of William Wordsworth*

from *The Prelude*, Book VI
—William Wordsworth

That very day,
From a bare ridge we also first beheld
Unveiled the summit of Mont Blanc, and grieved
To have a soulless image on the eye
 That had usurped upon a living thought
That never more could be. The wondrous Vale
Of Chamouny stretched far below, and soon
With its dumb cataracts and streams of ice,
A motionless array of mighty waves,
Five rivers broad and vast, made rich amends,
And reconciled us to realities;
There small birds warble from the leafy trees,
The eagle soars high in the element,
There doth the reaper bind the yellow sheaf,
The maiden spread the haycock in the sun,
While Winter like a well-tamed lion walks,
Descending from the mountain to make sport
Among the cottages by beds of flowers.

Whate'er in this wide circuit we beheld,
Or heard, was fitted to our unripe state
Of intellect and heart. With such a book
Before our eyes, we could not choose but read
Lessons of genuine brotherhood, the plain
And universal reason of mankind,
The truths of young and old. Nor, side by side
Pacing, two social pilgrims, or alone
Each with his humour, could we fail to abound
In dreams and fictions, pensively composed:
Dejection taken up for pleasure's sake,
And gilded sympathies, the willow wreath,
And sober posies of funereal flowers,
Gathered among those solitudes sublime
From formal gardens of the lady Sorrow,
Did sweeten many a meditative hour.

Yet still in me with those soft luxuries
Mixed something of stern mood, an underthirst
Of vigour seldom utterly allayed:
And from that source how different a sadness
Would issue, let one incident make known.
When from the Vallais we had turned, and clomb
Along the Simplon's steep and rugged road,
Following a band of muleteers, we reached
A halting-place, where all together took
Their noon-tide meal. Hastily rose our guide,
Leaving us at the board; awhile we lingered,
Then paced the beaten downward way that led
Right to a rough stream's edge, and there broke off;

The only track now visible was one
That from the torrent's further brink held forth
Conspicuous invitation to ascend
A lofty mountain. After brief delay
Crossing the unbridged stream, that road we took,
And clomb with eagerness, till anxious fears
Intruded, for we failed to overtake
Our comrades gone before. By fortunate chance,
While every moment added doubt to doubt,
A peasant met us, from whose mouth we learned
That to the spot which had perplexed us first
We must descend, and there should find the road,
Which in the stony channel of the stream
Lay a few steps, and then along its banks;
And, that our future course, all plain to sight,
Was downwards, with the current of that stream.
Loth to believe what we so grieved to hear,
For still we had hopes that pointed to the clouds,
We questioned him again, and yet again;
But every word that from the peasant's lips
Came in reply, translated by our feelings,
Ended in this,—'that we had crossed the Alps'.

Imagination—here the Power so called
Through sad incompetence of human speech,
That awful Power rose from the mind's abyss
Like an unfathered vapour that enwraps,
At once, some lonely traveller. I was lost;
Halted without an effort to break through;
But to my conscious soul I now can say—
"I recognise thy glory:" in such strength
Of usurpation, when the light of sense
Goes out, but with a flash that has revealed
The invisible world, doth greatness make abode,
There harbours; whether we be young or old,
Our destiny, our being's heart and home,
Is with infinitude, and only there;
With hope it is, hope that can never die,
Effort, and expectation, and desire,
And something evermore about to be.
Under such banners militant, the soul
Seeks for no trophies, struggles for no spoils
That may attest her prowess, blest in thoughts
That are their own perfection and reward,
Strong in herself and in beatitude
That hides her, like the mighty flood of Nile
Poured from his fount of Abyssinian clouds
To fertilise the whole Egyptian plain.

The Immortals
—Stephen Edgar

A breeze fills up the manna gum's huge lung,
That hologram of bronchioles. It sways there
Tethered and shifting like a hot-air balloon
Preparing for some fresh and doomed attempt
To circle the great globe. Heaped at its base
The litter of shed bark and collapsed boughs,
So much dumped ballast. Across an expanse of lawn—
The cat's savanna—a drowsing figure slouched
In an easy chair inhabits "Summertime",
Living by emptying this gap of day:
A straw hat on her face like a cartoon peon,
Her right arm limply draped over the side,
Jehovah's index finger pointing down
To where, half lost in the long grass, Daniel
Deronda's lying in *Daniel Deronda*,
His pages palping at the air, as though
Blindly taking in what it all is like.

It *is* hard to imagine. The shallow bay
Offers up to the light the illusory depths
Of a table buffed and polished to a lustre,
Except where an inlet-wide, flung net of wind
Hauls at the panicked shoals of chop and dazzle.
High up the sky is pale as faded denim
Worn through in a few frayed clouds, but where it comes
To earth, a cyan heavier than air
And not to breathe. And sometimes in the evening
The whole space thinks again, and sky and sea
Lie in each other's mirror, robed in gold
And self-absorbed against the envious land
They leach away, but for some failing islet
Or bluff that barely makes its presence felt.

Look, on her hand's back are the clues to grief,
Whatever she may think—those patches like
The remnants of a suntan, veins as blue
As any sky could wish, swollen through skin
As beautiful as birch bark, and as frail—
The emblems of a loss that will see out
The ending of the world.

Persisting in some region of obtuse
Sublimity, and full of an inhuman,
Distant pity, he'll contemplate her, baffled,
Then turn away perhaps like Beatrice
With her doubt-tainted smile. But he'll be there.

*

The heat is a dimension now, like time,
And as improbable. The cottage floats,
Not quite convinced it's happening, with its flies
And cracked linoleum, its shelves of books
Unaltered since the war, its bush-rat droppings,
The clocklike clicking of the roof—all tethered
To the least twitching of her dreaming fingers,
Her shallow breath. Later, before her friends
Descend, she'll wander barefoot through the rooms
In something easy with an ice-filled glass
And put some music on and watch the sea.

Early Ambition
—Paul Hetherington

It was to climb the knotted rope that hung
over the brown folds of the wrinkling river
nearly as high as the holding branch, to fall
forwards, and to straighten, so the body
became a missile, aimed at the turbid hole
between rocks and river bank, then to enter
water with an easy grace, a diver
heading through the gut-thrilling air
into the channel where frothing currents siphoned
rapidly into the quieter water
that saw the river turn towards the city.
It was to put drowned Andrew out of mind—
all of us had cheered
his antics on the rope a hundred times.

Catastrophe Poem

THEME:	man-made catastrophe
FORM:	3 sestets
RHYME SCHEME:	none
METRE:	none
POEM LENGTH:	18 lines

FORM:
— 1st sestet = exposition > beginning "What I know . . ."
— 2nd sestet = conflict > beginning "What I don't know . . ."
— 3rd sestet = climax > beginning "What I don't want to know . . ."

TASK:
— select a man-made catastrophe, for example:
  war
  invasion
  genocide
  oil spill
  deforestation
  displacement
  arson
— consider humanity's cultural/political role in event
— write yourself into event > create visual/psychological memories
— catastrophe may be treated as metaphor for inner human state

READING:
— Jack Davis 'Mining Company's Hymn' *Penguin Anthology of Australian Poetry*
— Anthony Hecht 'The Book of Yolek' (30-line sestina) *Poets Laureate Anthology*
— Edward Vance Palmer 'The Farmer Remembers the Somme' *Penguin Anthology of Australian Poetry*
— Elizabeth Riddell 'The Children March' *P&W Anthology of Australian Poetry*
— Peter Skrzynecki 'Migrant Hostel' *Penguin Anthology of Australian Poetry*
— Colin Thiele 'Radiation Victim' *Penguin Anthology of Australian Poetry*
— Chris Wallace-Crabbe 'Other People' *P&W Anthology of Australian Poetry*
— Sam Wagan Watson 'for the wake and skeleton dance' *P&W Anthology of Australian Poetry*

The Farmer Remembers the Somme
—Edward Vance Palmer

Will they never fade or pass!
    The mud, and the misty figures endlessly coming
In file through the foul morass,
And the grey flood-water lipping the reeds and grass,
    And the steel wings drumming.

The hills are bright in the sun:
    There's nothing changed or marred in the well-known places:
When work for the day is done
There's talk, and quiet laughter, and gleams of fun
    On the old folks' faces.

I have returned to these:
    The farm, and the kindly bush, and the young calves lowing:
But all that my mind sees
Is a quaking bog in a mist—stark, snapped trees,
    And the dark Somme flowing.

The Children March
—Elizabeth Riddell

The children of the world are on the march
From the dangerous cots, the nurseries ringed with fire,
The poisoned toys, the playgrounds pitted
With bomb craters and shrapnel strewn about;
From the whips, the iron bars, the guns' great shout,
The malevolent teachers and the lethal sports
Played on the ruined fields fenced by red wires.

The children of the world are on the march
With the doll and the school-bag to safe quarters,
The temporary haven, the impermanent home;
Nightly turning their thoughts to the forsaken hearth,
The wandering, wondering children of the world
March on the sea and land and crowded air—
The unsmiling sons, the sad bewildered daughters.

Cento Poem

THEME:	as deemed by cento line
FORM:	3 quintains
RHYME SCHEME:	optional
METRE:	optional

BACKGROUND:
— 'cento' from Latin *cento* (patchwork)
— Homer as major source (Greek literature)
    see Trygaeus > adaptation of lines from *The Iliad* & *The Odyssey*
    also *Homerokentrones* (Byzantine period)
— Virgil as major source (later Roman times)
    see Hosidius Geta > *Medea*
    also Proba > *Virgilanus*

FORM:
— full cento poem completely composed of lines from work by other poet/s
— lines are reordered/reorganised for new effect
— semi-cento poem incorporates one or more lines from other poet/s
— traditionally method of homage *or* satire
— quintain = 5-line stanza

TASK:
— select *one* line from a poem by a past poet
— use this line to dictate subject/tone of your poem
— utilise line as final line in each quintain
— cento line may be italicised, parenthesised, placed within quotation marks, indented
— cento line may also appear as though naturally part of text proper > hidden
— ensure accuracy of quoted line
— cite source at bottom of page > do not plagiarise by default!
— include 'cento' in title > indication of 'borrowing' to reader

READING:
— Jordie Albiston 'mandragora' > the Bible, Browning, Byron, Coleridge, Congreve, Donne, Keats, McCrae, Milton, Shakespeare, Sidney, Swinburne, Wordsworth *the sonnet according to 'm'*
— T.S. Eliot 'The Fire Sermon' (section 3 from 'The Wasteland') > Edmund Spenser 'Prothalamion' *Norton Anthology of Poetry*
— David Musgrave 'The Swimmer: A Cento' > Byron, Shelley, Slessor, Swinburne, Tennyson, Tuckerman, et al *Phantom Limb*
— Michael Sharkey 'Where the Bunyip Builds its Nest: Five Centos' > 200 lines from almost 200 Australian poets *Another Fine Morning in Paradise*
— Alex Skovron 'No Highway' > John Masefield 'The Return' (from *The Wanderer*) & Nevil Shute *No Highway* (epigraph) *Infinite City*

No Highway
—Alex Skovron

Everything hurts
There is no place to hide
A glance into the glass to listen to his lines
A glance into the mirror: it molests his gaze
He never could outstare himself without blinking
So few clues on his battlefield face

The eyes italicize what he is thinking
(The way to go shall glimmer in the mind)
But everything hurts: there is no hiding-place
The roman sun is sinking

Where the Bunyip Builds its Nest: Five Centos
—Michael Sharkey

1. This Happy Isle

And shall thy joyous lays no more be heard?
What songs were they the Sirens sung?
Against the shade-side of a bending gum
they chain us two by two, and whip and lash along.
We will not join the general groan,
O barren land! O blank bright day!
O hopeless wilderness without one fruit,
what words are left for Hope to say?

Happiest work of finest Hand!
Huge kangaroos, grotesque and grey,
here, where we carelessly stroll today,
may shine hereafter from these songless days.
The magpie sitteth silently,
above us spreads the brightening sky—
How nobly dost thou rise above all forms
O Intellect! without thee, what were life?

Where the platypus twists and doubles,
and grass upon the trees is found,
the singers with their time-sticks rang,
saw the corroboree's measured dance,
the wombat and the kangaroo,
the creeks whereby the lyre-birds sing—
the placid river winding by,
soft hills behind, the sea before.

I had not thought again to see
forsaken home and burial mound.

We see all good things disappear—
the very best a scabby lamb;
I doubt if aught so great e'er fell so far.
Far too many like you have been taken.
Others have sung the self-same song.
'Have you done?' I say, 'Let us go'.

2. Drought and Doctrine

The creeks are dry, and many rivers too,
and the steer will go down to be sold for his hide.
When earth so poor a banquet makes,
dust, dung, and broken herbage fly.
Where the dingo should be seen, sounds the Army tambourine,
and there is no Up the Country for us now.
There is fondling of the idol that they love the best on earth,
and from the forest, prayers, and incense rise.

Between hot mouldering banks, it came to this—
where the curlews shriek and the gum trees wave.
Of course we ain't all sheep—there must be goats.
Can this be where the hovel stood?
And sluggish teams, that crept along the road:
why should I babble? Let me lie
by still lagoons, and mark the flight
of all animals most to be pitied

A score of years has taken flight;
shall we stay and never venture?
Courage to dare, and the strength to endure:
The track of life is sometimes smooth, at other times 'tis rough.
She kissed him thrice on his sunburnt brow;
Gold! supreme is thy dominion,
Little wonder that she loved him,
Geordie struck it rich at last.

A pleasant land is the land of dreams,
a bar of an old-fashioned waltz!
A lady in her boudoir stands before a faded carte,
and the pain of the past it is past.
Her life is lovely. Stream, and wind and bird,
the charm of flowers, the wealth of fruit;
how many springs have passed since then?
The growing crops all wave and dance.

3. The Common Trench

Education and English polish are very unsaleable stuff.
(When will the world be sea, and pure?)
Awake, O fat boy! leave somniferous things—
our swords from their scabbards will start and blush red,

and wits are dropping one by one.
The diggers are digging, and digging deep.
Fried potatoes is a dish—
we have lectures on popular themes.

Not yet her day. How long 'Not Yet?'…
since I was a tiny shaver.
They woke me from dreaming in the dawn of the day,
'Twere an excellent thing to fight
Ring out, for the Lord of Hosts shall reign
and not the poor disciplined people!
He chooses you to be His rod
and Battle-axe of Justice wield.

Are our lies theirs, and our truth their truth?
Join hands—all malice be forgot—
One of these poets—which is it?—somewhere or another sings
there comes a point where we will not yield, no matter if right or wrong;
the old, old faiths must falter, and the old, old creeds must fail—
The strongest feet may slip in blood!
A kiss, a twisted smile, a sigh,
when did the good Postmaster die?

Debarred from joining the rank and file,
there's little else a woman can do,
'Slip one, purl one, decrease to seven'—
We cried, 'How long!' We sighed, 'Not Yet!
For them no trumpet sounds the call, no poet plies his art.
The parson came and brought the news last night.
She was a widow, and she read
What's grief but the after-blindness?

Over the corn I heard, to-day,
In the matter of turning the cheek
Will you stand idle, with battles unwon?
An' a string of dirty insults on 'is tongue.
'Would I could go to Egypt to my son.'
'That was a long while ago', she said,
We'll have another storm, I think'—
The wisdom of our strength comes very slow.

4. Galah Song: Dance, Little Wombat

Ahab within, mad master of my craft,
I dreamed of fame and in my folly went,
probing dim caverns of the Nullarbor.
believing that I can explain the mysteries of life
Flower gyrating in a verbose bowl,
if I opened the door to the lift,
we'll have all gone off fishing, or to the pub.
I'm sure I wouldn't care to be Lord Mayor of a city like ours.

and you, murderer with the matchbox,
a sad dementia from the past
plying knives and forks with a peek-in sound, with a tuck-in sound,
you want big-big Bunyip get you?
I have never spoken of your nakedness
by the bushes in the creek,
a thin being with a sharp nose and a strong reek
with the gestures of Moses, and a white cockatoo.

See how the floor of Heav'n is thick
where Sidney Nolan, like a looney don
sprang to a height, fire-sinewed in the dark,
and gave it to you, lying on the stable floor,
zig-zagged till our eyes were sore,
and Vasco Nunez de Balboa heard.
Will the dribbling moon kill me now?
Reveille sounded at the bedroom door.

So all men come at last to their Explorer's Tree
and still no little cloud, no eulowirree.
My lady Anne smiled in the gallery,
she was over a hundred, easy,
queer little deep brown almond eyes
warm to hold as the butcher-bird.
We were not lovers. We hadn't time.
There's an old dope living in a field of fowls.

Knowing only the dark husbandry of roots,
I set down my swag. Against the sunset
I showed them the sweet land of Jimbin,
saw their sardines slipping out of state hatcheries,
and laughed and hummed a chantey:
'The guttural goose hath ushered in the day'.
The great red kangaroos bounce in the air
Like a rivet through the hand.

5. In Zero Gravity

Golf at the weekend, gardening after five,
each esky must contain a peach,
Saturday morning, and a few of us gather,
some go mad, begin to see inwardly;
even the cemetery dead partake
of this land of half-past nine.
The Catholic Lending Library is warm
Time is a cellar where all the wine's been drunk,

What do you think about when you are seventy-eight, '
among the vapours of neutrality?
—Shall we sing those songs now? Remember them?
Time to hang up the gloves? That's time to kill.
Blink, blink. HOSPITAL. SILENCE.

You do not feel so well today?
Here is some *strange writing* hidden away in an old book;
the minnow class swims in

Who owns this voice? Who speaks?
All that I know about poetry is that it has
Familiar compound ghosts? No,
linen folded for the future:
iambics chide industrialists
and vanish in the gentle air.
Mild forgotten poems
drop their kiddies at the kindy.

Outside, FJs are dragging up the street,
and now my wife is in the car,
I could write an ode to Steve,
i read his poems / & he read
Mrs Russell Viney nee McNab!
This mix is right for poetry.
A breeze picks out a damp patch.
It was warmer than this in the cave.

I'll try. I'll try. But it is hard to be scattered.
Drunk at the time, & Vietnam,
& yes, life's an Australian movie just now, no plot.
See how far I've come?
Enjoy that ice cream Gerald,
friend of bob,
there really has to be a limit.
Time will show us up as lunatics.

In some ways, I believe as my neighbours
that I've been here too long,
a camera   self directed   flashed links
in a national geographic
impulse to ignore frivolity and to be really serious.
Have you made me up as well?
They were all poets, so the poets said.
Think on me kindly.

If I don't discontinue straight away,
I'll grow large in Tibet, transmorph to Dakini:
yarnevano/ wotyarfind/ downther/ people
psychopomp and ceremony
[formless? paradox of construction—
Socrates said when our feet hurt we hurt all over.
My way is I make a huge fuss and then I get over it.
Lines I improve, boundaries erode

Childhood Poem

THEME:	early memory
FORM:	structural relationship to content
RHYME SCHEME:	optional
METRE:	optional
POEM LENGTH:	maximum 13 lines

FORM:

— design structure to visually reflect/complement event

> see Jenkins' pre-lingual block poem (unformed)

> see White's final tercet following 7 sestets (children mid-air on trampoline or jumping 'up' into heaven)

TASK:

— choose a childhood memory focussing on one particular sense:

sight

taste

sound

smell

touch

(motion)

— inhabit childhood world *parallel* to adult experience

— endeavour to evoke the 'always now' of childhood

— use specific detail/imagery for colour

— attempt interplay between internal perception & external environment

READING:

— Robert Adamson 'My Tenth Birthday' *The Golden Bird*

— Peter Boyle 'Paralysis (1955)' *Towns in the Great Desert*

— John Muk Muk Burke 'The Headmaster' *New Music*

— Michelle Cahill 'Childhood' *Vishvarupa*

— Robert Harris 'Six Years Old' *Australian Poetry Since 1788*

— Terry Jaensch 'Swing' *New Music*

— John Jenkins 'I am Making Noises in the Sun' *Growing up with Mr Menzies*

— James McAuley 'Childhood Morning—Homebush' *P&W Anthology of Australian Poetry*

— Pi O 'The Paper Round' *Australian Poetry Since 1788*

— Vicki Raymond 'Don't Talk About Your Childhood' *Australian Poetry Since 1788*

— Petra White 'Trampolining' *A Hunger*

Paralysis (1955)
—Peter Boyle

Laid out flat
in the back of the station wagon my father borrowed
I look up:
the leaves are immense,
green and golden with clear summer light
breaking through—
though I turn only my neck
I can see all of them
along this avenue that has no limits.

What does it matter
that I am only eyes
if I am to be carried
so lightly
under the trees of the world?
From beyond the numbness of my strange body
the wealth of the leaves
falls forever
into my small still watching.

My Tenth Birthday
—Robert Adamson

We went to Pumpkin Point
for my tenth birthday

the best picnic beach on the river

the mud is thinner
and doesn't smell as off

and there is a swing
made from a huge truck tyre

I wore my first jeans
and got a cane rod and a bird book

Dad washed the rabbit blood
out of the back of his truck
and we spread blankets
and pillows over the splinters

A storm came up after lunch
and I cut my foot open
on a sardine can as I ran into a cave

it was the same cave
I found again four years later
on a night my father set out the nets

and slept beside me
for the only time in his life

Childhood
—Michelle Cahill

The afternoon cruises,
after badminton, lemonade
and chutney sandwiches.
Voices are like ribbon made
for unwrapping the past.
Syllables of imaginary laughter
blend with the real, as I recall
the warmth of uncles, aunts, cousins
left behind in foreign cities,
Mumbai, London, Goa.
I think of the bright day when dad
flew our kite on Primrose Hill.
It's hard to say what matters.
Everything fragments,
defers to time's calibrations,
the long shadows are deceptive.

I piggy-back my daughter
in summer's leaf-light.
We swim laps in tandem
riding a pink foam noodle, sinking fast,
her tiny arms a choker for my neck.
I'm weak to her commands, her tears.
In any competition, I must lose.
The dragonfly's flight is a tease
never kissing its reflection,
a cross-stitch lacing the pool.
The distant hum of the freeway
sounds like a hole in the heart,
the softest turbulence.
The garden is a green humidicrib.

Swing
—Terry Jaensch

I am swinging
rushing toward the
tree tops

impressing the sky
with my heels
my toes—ten

frequent fliers
forgetting
my father

the bar of blood
that cracked
my cheek

my meal
this morning
left—sitting

I am swinging
packing into
each pocket

each underdog
return—each runt
to his litter of fists

I am swinging
singing castrato
thrilling in endless

vowels—lamenting
the lean wicked leg
killing sensation

Opera Seria
is swinging
D above high C

alarm bells ringing
Da Capo!
Da Capo!

I am prodigal
returning
religiously shamed

by my faith
in those closest
to me—I am standing

clock faced
in a corner
pendulum swinging

sounding
each hour long
approach

at the instant
struck dumb
hiding

in my hands
the dial of
days

the frequency
of my
father

City Poem

THEME: a city
FORM: sestets
RHYME SCHEME: abcdad
METRE: none
POEM LENGTH: 3 stanzas

FORM:
—   title = name of city
—   compose poem in 6-line stanzas
—   utilise name of city as final word of each stanza > recurring mantra
      (NB: this will affect rhyme scheme . . .)

TASK:
—   compose a poem exploring your city of choice
—   poem may be positive/negative/celebratory/humorous/nostalgic/other (choose &
      maintain approach)
—   concentrate on *description* as process
—   employ imagery as dominant poetic impulse
      'imagery' related to 'imitation' > likeness/copy/resemblance/reflection
—   think like a journalist > find 'an angle'
—   evoke inner being of city through imagery
—   sustain cultural/historical/political/environmental/visual precision
—   treat subject as (almost) human > bring city to life

READING:
—   William Blake 'London' *Seven Centuries*
—   J. Brenchley 'Odorous Melbourne' *Penguin Anthology of Australian Poetry*
—   Michelle Cahill 'Ode to Mumbai' *Contemporary Asian Australian Poets*
—   Dan Disney 'Collins Street, 5pm' *and then when the*
—   John Forbes 'Sydney' *Collected Poems*
—   Philip Hodgins 'Melbourne Heatwave' *New Music*
—   Ee Tiang Hong 'Perth' *Contemporary Asian Australian Poets*
—   John Mateer 'Johannesburg' *Barefoot Speech*
—   Jacob Rosenberg 'Vienna' *New Music*
—   Ouyang Yu 'Moon Over Melbourne' *Penguin Anthology of Australian Poetry*
—   Fay Zwicky 'Losing Track' *New Music*

London
—William Blake

I wander thro' each charter'd street,
Near where the charter'd Thames does flow.
And mark in every face I meet
Marks of weakness, marks of woe.

In every cry of every Man,
In every Infants cry of fear,
In every voice: in every ban,
The mind-forg'd manacles I hear

How the Chimney-sweepers cry
Every blackning Church appalls,
And the hapless Soldiers sigh
Runs in blood down Palace walls

But most thro' midnight streets I hear
How the youthful Harlots curse
Blasts the new-born Infants tear
And blights with plagues the Marriage hearse

Odorous Melbourne
—J. Brenchley

Odorous Melbourne, city of stinks!
What fragrance o'erhovers thy cesspools and sinks;—
I have smelt many smells, but the richest *per se*,
May justly be claim'd, luscious Melbourne, by thee.
When the sun has gone down, and the wind's in the west,
And the night-air is heavy, by closeness opprest,
From thy fam'd open drains, a soft essence is thrown,
An odour delightful, uniquely thine own.
    Odorous Melbourne—delectable Melbourne!
    Odoriferous Melbourne—sweet Stinkomalee!

Cologne may boast proudly—that sanctified town
Of the forty odd stinks that enhance its renown;
But thine has a raciness rivall'd by none,
Like all the full forty commingled in one.
And though time-honour'd odours pervade the Fleet Ditch,
With its full-flavour'd mud and perfumeries rich,
Let them boast as they may: to this creed I incline,
It is not a patch on these brave drains of thine.
    Odorous Melbourne—delectable Melbourne!
    Odoriferous Melbourne—soft Stinkomalee!

Coming of Age Poem

THEME:	defining adolescent moment
FORM:	tercets
RHYME SCHEME:	abc/dec/fgc/etc.
METRE:	none
POEM LENGTH:	maximum 15 lines
STANCE:	1st person singular ("I")

FORM:
— utilise 3-line stanzas as stepping-stones along path of self-development

TASK:
— choose event in adolescence that deeply altered you *or* imagine event in terms of adopted persona (see Leonard Cohen lyrics)
— concentrate on change in understanding/insight that occurred
— describe process in terms of *internal* awareness via *external* incident
— action > reaction
— imply sense of 'new' adulthood (positive or negative)
— the getting of wisdom/cynicism/education
— depict moment of enlightenment:
announcement
confession
revelation
wake-up call
rude shock
instruction
witness
retribution
praise
— make your poem sing with profound/'biblical' power

READING:
— Elizabeth Bishop 'In the Waiting Room' *The Complete Poems*
— Leonard Cohen 'Story of Isaac' *Concise Leonard Cohen*
— Diane Fahey 'Thirteen' *New Music*
— Jennifer Harrison 'Electra' *P&W Anthology of Australian Poetry*
— Gwen Harwood 'Father and Child: Barn Owl' *Mappings of the Plane*
— Tony Lintermans 'The Escape from Youth' *P&W Anthology of Australian Poetry*
— Les Murray 'Spring Hail' *Collected Poems*
— Peter Rose 'Donatello in Wangaratta' *Macquarie PEN Anthology*
— Robyn Rowland 'Coming of Age' *The Road South*
— Dylan Thomas 'Fern Hill' *Norton Anthology of Poetry*

Father and Child: Barn Owl
—Gwen Harwood

Daybreak: the household slept.
I rose, blessed by the sun.
A horny fiend, I crept
out with my father's gun.
Let him dream of a child
obedient, angel-mild—

old No-Sayer, robbed of power
by sleep. I knew my prize
who swooped home at this hour
with daylight-riddled eyes
to his place on a high beam
in our old stables, to dream

light's useless time away.
I stood, holding my breath,
in urine-scented hay,
master of life and death,
a wisp-haired judge whose law
would punish beak and claw.

My first shot struck. He swayed,
ruined, beating his only
wing, as I watched, afraid
by the fallen gun, a lonely
child who believed death clean
and final, not this obscene

bundle of stuff that dropped,
and dribbled through loose straw
tangling in bowels, and hopped
blindly closer. I saw
those eyes that did not see
mirror my cruelty

while the wrecked thing that could
not bear the light nor hide
hobbled in its own blood.
My father reached my side,
gave me the fallen gun.
"End what you have begun."

I fired. The blank eyes shone
once into mine, and slept.
I leaned my head upon
my father's arm, and wept,
owl-blind in early sun
for what I had begun.

In the Waiting Room
—Elizabeth Bishop

In Worcester, Massachusetts,
I went with Aunt Consuelo
to keep her dentist's appointment
and sat and waited for her
in the dentist's waiting room.
It was winter. It got dark
early. The waiting room
was full of grown-up people,
arctics and overcoats,
lamps and magazines.
My aunt was inside
what seemed like a long time
and while I waited I read
the *National Geographic*
(I could read) and carefully
studied the photographs:
the inside of a volcano,
black, and full of ashes;
then it was spilling over
in rivulets of fire.
Osa and Martin Johnson
dressed in riding breeches,
laced boots, and pith helmets.
A dead man slung on a pole
—"Long Pig," the caption said.
Babies with pointed heads
wound round and round with string;
black, naked women with necks
wound round and round with wire
like the necks of light bulbs.
Their breasts were horrifying.
I read it right straight through.
I was too shy to stop.
And then I looked at the cover:
the yellow margins, the date.

Suddenly, from inside,
came an *oh!* of pain
—Aunt Consuelo's voice—
not very loud or long.
I wasn't at all surprised;
even then I knew she was
a foolish, timid woman.
I might have been embarrassed,
but wasn't. What took me
completely by surprise
was that it was *me*:
my voice, in that mouth.
Without thinking at all

I was my foolish aunt,
I—we—were falling, falling,
our eyes glued to the cover
of the *National Geographic*,
February, 1918.

I said to myself: three days
and you'll be seven years old.
I was saying it to stop
the sensation of falling off
the round, turning world
into cold, blue-black space.
But I felt: you are an *I*,
you are an *Elizabeth*,
you are one of *them*.
Why should you be one, too?
I scarcely dared to look
to see what it was I was.
I gave a sidelong glance
—I couldn't look any higher—
at shadowy gray knees,
trousers and skirts and boots
and different pairs of hands
lying under the lamps.
I knew that nothing stranger
had ever happened, that nothing
stranger could ever happen.

Why should I be my aunt,
or me, or anyone?
What similarities—
boots, hands, the family voice
I felt in my throat, or even
the *National Geographic*
and those awful hanging breasts—
held us all together
or made us all just one?
How—I didn't know any
word for it—how "unlikely" . . .
How had I come to be here,
like them, and overhear
a cry of pain that could have
got loud and worse but hadn't?

The waiting room was bright
and too hot. It was sliding
beneath a big black wave,
another, and another.

Then I was back in it.
The War was on. Outside,
in Worcester, Massachusetts,
were night and slush and cold,

and it was still the fifth
of February, 1918.

Thirteen
—Diane Fahey

I was practising being a saint.
My brown lace-ups were clamped
to the dusty floor, and I was in them.
The mirror, an oval drop
of flat untrembling water, showed
a pale girl inside a yellow raincoat.
I hated it. 'This one,' I said.
My mother passed the silky beige one,
the dearer one, back to the woman,
and softly they agreed: 'Too young
to know its value.'
　　　　　　'Some of us even
wear yellow raincoats to school!'
The nun stood on a bench—
wasp-waisted, her cheeks covered
with tributaries of red lightning.
Her eyes glittered as two hundred girls
marched with military precision
round the playground. In tune
with a deeper instinct, I dragged
my feet into the asphalt,
waiting to be detected, punished . . .
She was the one who ground me down
the way she ground her yellow teeth,
and almost triumphed—
until the day when, kindled with rage,
she struck me across the arm:
'Get out, then!' And I had won,
my eyes drops of flat untrembling water,
giving her back her hatred,
polishing it with the fresh shine of youth.

The Escape from Youth
—Tony Lintermans

My father's discipline closed me like a box.
A hardness hammered shut the lid.
For fifteen years, no matter what he did,
I was unreachable. Venom sealed the locks.

Neutral beauty kept me company. Walking
through neighbours' cattle, from moving skies and trees
I learnt the slower vaster intimacies.
Avoiding the world of men, I stopped talking,

except intensely to myself. Rumours
of happiness sometimes seeped outside the box.
'Untrue!' I howled, and double-checked the locks.
In the dark, poetry grew like a tumour.

When the poems were big enough to break
their way out, dragging me behind, I saw
my father's face, more bitten than before,
a soft fist eaten by love, impossible to hate.

There is no forgiveness now, nor the need.
Silence bred rich fruits—a known self, those skies—
for which I thank my father. Amnesia lies
behind our peace. Neither of us dares to bleed.

Communal Poem

THEME:	public/community event
FORM:	2 octaves
RHYME SCHEME:	none
METRE:	none
STANCE:	1st person plural ("we")
TENSE:	past

FORM:

— set 1st octave (8-line stanza) 'before' event, 2nd section 'after' event

— 1st octave beginning "When we arrived . . ."

2nd octave beginning "When we left . . ."

or

1st octave beginning "While we slept . . ."

2nd octave beginning "When we awoke . . ."

— compose both octaves in past tense, for example:

"the tree *stood*", "the phone *rang*", "we *saw*"

— employ plural "we" > individual poet as vocal representative of group

— having decided on subject, *do not* mention as such in poem > dance around (for example: "that fateful September day" rather than "9/11")

— add title specific to event on completion of poem:

'The Great Depression'

'Dokkoon's Baby'

'Earthquake in Chile'

TASK:

— write a poem in reaction to a public event, for example:

first moon landing

Sorry Day

Black Saturday

tsunami

dismantling of Berlin Wall

Easter/Ramadan/Yom Kippur/festival

election/assassination

declaration of peace

READING:

— Robert Adamson 'Canticle for the Bicentennial Dead' *P&W Anthology of Australian Poetry*

— Adam Aitken 'S 21' *P&W Anthology of Australian Poetry*

— Lisa Bellear 'Women's Liberation' *Penguin Anthology of Australian Poetry*

— W.T. Goodge 'Federation' *P&W Anthology of Australian Poetry*

— Ian McBryde 'The West Gate' *Flank*

— Morgan Yasbincek 'nineleven' *P&W Anthology of Australian Poetry*

— Fay Zwicky 'Tiananmen Square June 4, 1989' *P&W Anthology of Australian Poetry*

Federation
—W.T. Goodge

Let us sing of Federation
      ('T is the theme of every cult)
And the joyful expectation
      Of its ultimate result.
'Twill confirm the jubilation
Of protection's expectation,
And the quick consolidation
Of freetrade with every nation;
And teetotal legislation
Will achieve its consummation
And increase our concentration
On the art of bibulation.
We shall drink to desperation,
And be quite the soberest nation
We'll be desperately loyal
Unto everything that's royal,
And be ultrademocratic
In a matter most emphatic.
We'll be prosperous and easeful,
And pre-eminently peaceful,
And we'll take our proper station
As a military nation!
We shall show the throne affection,
Also sever the connection,
And the bonds will get no Fainter
And we'll also cut the painter.
We'll proclaim with lute and tabor
The millennium of labour,
And we'll bow before the gammon
Of plutocracy and Mammon.
We'll adopt all fads and fictions
And their mass of contradictions
If all hopes are consummated
When Australia's federated;
For the Federation speeches
This one solid moral teach us—
That a pile of paradoxes are expected to result!

S 21
—Adam Aitken

Of what will they dream?
Which song will they remember? What name
will they want to name—the bones—in their darkness?
—Mario Licón Cabrera, *Osario*

The way—ideally—we might remember:
a glass case or a neat Perspex tower
of skulls and thighbones.
Blood and rust melded together
in the springs of an old French style bed base.
An old cartridge case shit can.
Samplers of jumbled DNA,
a room of ragged cast-offs.
How to come away from it,
to photograph it, how long to stay there and stare
at the spattered tiles and the ripped out wiring.
To wonder what endless days
reading an archive of ten thousand 'confessions'
does for the eyes; I'm sick of questions
no-one wants to answer.
A forensic display of bullet wound trauma,
all logic and angles
is somehow a relief.

In the schoolyard recanters stacked up
end on end, queued for each device, machines
no theory committee
could calibrate to perfection.
Lies, half-truths, false leads, endless plot.
To write 'my life is not worth a bullet'
concludes more than narrative.
How to sign off a letter
with terror's salutations—and after that?
'Ahhrgh' perhaps, or a dog's whimper,
or a dragging chain.
Someone who'd been to Belsen
had written 'Justice' in the visitor's book.
But this was a rustic and ham-fisted machine
with no industrial prototype.
I too have to write, wondering where I am
on the chain-link of paranoia
connecting a tyrant to a farmer's son
who was handy with a shovel;
someone like the accountant across the corridor
doing the company's credit/debit sheet—
the guy with *all* the stories, who
knew how to file, the one who said
he'd done his job protecting his nation
with a few blunt instruments

a fountain pen, and a beautiful signature.

nineleven
—Morgan Yasbincek

when she was woken, told about the planes
the scenarios would not gather

she realised she had been hit, her collapsed spine televised
from circulating helicopters

she had time for a short call on her mobile before she was:

sucked out of a window, tossed into a livid blue sky

jammed into a stairwell with thousands of hands, hands and smoke

wading through ash and dust, scooping it out of her ears, mouth, eyes,
coughing it onto her clothes

queuing to give blood, lighting candles

digging for three nights without sleep

sitting on the aircraft trying to remember the emergency procedure;
oxygen, life jacket, the toggles, the whistle

Concrete Poem

THEME: open
FORM: visual representation
RHYME SCHEME: none
METRE: none
POEM LENGTH: maximum one page

BACKGROUND:
—   'pattern poetry' (also 'shaped poetry') 1700BC Crete/700BC Egypt
—   also Japan/India
—   'concrete' term specific to 1950s/1960s > afterwards referred to as 'visual poetry'

FORM:
—   see altar poem & *carmen figuratum*
—   common shapes > crucifix/chalice/column/sun/geometric designs
—   object to present poem in particular shape relating to subject matter: pictorial typography
—   shape may be literal, abstract, or combination (for example: replace text with own words on text-based item such as ticket/menu/receipt)
—   poem may be written on paper/glass/stone/wood/other material
—   difficult form to accomplish with success
—   subtlety of technique (Apollinaire *Calligrammes* 1918)
—   notable experimentation since WWII (Ian Hamilton Finlay/Ernst Jandl)

TASK:
—   consider relationship between words & visual arrangement on page
—   seek happy marriage between content & form
—   avoid visuals completely dominating meaning of poem
—   construct concrete poem (limit one page)

READING:
—   Guillaume Apollinaire *Calligrammes*
—   Kate Fagan 'Concrete Poem' *Penguin Anthology of Australian Poetry*
—   Toby Fitch 'Rawshock' *Rawshock*
—   George Herbert 'Easter Wings' *Norton Anthology of Poetry*
—   John Hollander 'Swan and Shadow' *Norton Anthology of Poetry*
—   David Kelly *Book*
—   Alan Riddell 'Recessional' *Australian Poetry Since 1788*
—   Alex Selenitsch 'Weeds' *Australian Poetry Since 1788*
—   George Starbuck 'Sonnet in the Shape of a Potted Christmas Tree' *The Works*

Easter Wings
—George Herbert

Lord, who createdst man in wealth and store,
Though foolishly he lost the same,
Decaying more and more
Till he became
Most poor:
With thee
O let me rise
As larks, harmoniously,
And sing this day thy victories:
Then shall the fall further the flight in me.

My tender age in sorrow did begin;
And still with sicknesses and shame
Thou didst so punish sin,
That I became
Most thin.
With thee
Let me combine,
And feel this day thy victory;
For, if I imp my wing on thine,
Affliction shall advance the flight in me.

Sonnet in the Shape of a Potted Christmas Tree
—George Starbuck

*

O
fury-
bedecked!
O glitter-torn!
Let the wild wind erect
bonbonbonanzas; junipers affect
frostyfreeze turbans; iciclestuff adorn
all cuckolded creation in a madcap crown of horn!
It's a new day; no scapegrace of a sect
tidying up the ashtrays playing Daughter-in-Law Elect;
bells! bibelots! popsicle cigars! shatter the glassware! a son born
now
now
while ox and ass and infant lie
together as poor creatures will
and tears of her exertion still
cling in the spent girl's eye
and a great firework in the sky
drifts to the western hill.

Dialogue Poem

THEME:	a conversation
FORM:	open/free
RHYME SCHEME:	none
METRE:	none
POEM LENGTH:	approximately 18 lines
TONE:	demotic/colloquial

FORM:
— devices to represent dialogue include:
    single quote marks
    double quote marks
    italics
    indents
    parentheses
— avoid bold
— plain text (no visual devices) may also be used . . .

TASK:
— write a poem consisting entirely of dialogue
— "he says/she says", "I asked/you answered", etc. permitted
— be consistent with chosen device (quote marks, italics, other)
— endeavour to *imply* situation without stating all facts
— endeavour to *imbibe* colloquy with atmosphere/forward motion
— build response upon response
— create interest/intrigue
— raise/twist/bend/truncate language: avoid pure prose
— conversational snippets allowed > eavesdropping
— may begin mid-conversation

READING:
— anonymous 'Lord Randall' *Norton Anthology of Poetry*
— W.H. Auden 'O What is That Sound' *Collected Poems*
— Rosemary Dobson 'The Conversation' *www.poetrylibrary.edu.au*
— Bob Dylan 'A Hard Rain's A-Gonna Fall' *www.bobdylan.com*
— Gwen Harwood 'Dialogue' *Penguin Anthology of Australian Poetry*
— John Kinsella 'Visitant Eclogue' *P&W Anthology of Australian Poetry*
— Sylvia Plath 'Dialogue Between Ghost and Priest' *www.poemhunter.com*
— Andrew Taylor 'The Gardener and His Garden: A Dialogue' *Penguin Anthology of Australian Poetry*
— Alan Wearne 'Legend: Jack, the barman, talks to Kim. Saturday, 6 June 1970, 1.15 a.m.' *P&W Anthology of Australian Poetry*

Lord Randall
—anonymous

"Oh where ha'e ye been, Lord Randall my son?
O where ha'e ye been, my handsome young man?"
    "I ha'e been to the wild wood: mother, make my bed soon,
    For I'm weary wi' hunting, and fain wald lie down."

"Where gat ye your dinner, Lord Randall my son?
Where gat ye your dinner, my handsome young man?"
    "I dined wi' my true love; mother, make my bed soon,
    For I'm weary wi' hunting, and fain wald lie down."

"What gat ye to your dinner, Lord Randall my son?
What gat ye to your dinner, my handsome young man?"
    "I gat eels boiled in broo: mother, make my bed soon,
    For I'm weary wi' hunting, and fain wald lie down."

"What became of your bloodhounds, Lord Randall my son?
What became of your bloodhounds, my handsome young man?"
    "O they swelled and they died: mother, make my bed soon,
    for I'm weary wi' hunting, and fain wald lie down."

"O I fear ye are poisoned, Lord Randall my son!
O I fear ye are poisoned, my handsome young man!"
    "O yes, I am poisoned: mother, make my bed soon,
    For I'm sick at the heart, and I fain wald lie down."

from A Hard Rain's A-Gonna Fall
—Bob Dylan

Oh, where have you been, my blue-eyed son?
Oh, where have you been, my darling young one?
I've stumbled on the side of twelve misty mountains
I've walked and I've crawled on six crooked highways
I've stepped in the middle of seven sad forests
I've been out in front of a dozen dead oceans
I've been ten thousand miles in the mouth of a graveyard
And it's a hard, and it's a hard, it's a hard, and it's a hard
And it's a hard rain's a-gonna fall

from *The Lovemakers*
Legend: Jack, the barman, talks to Kim. Saturday, June 6 1970, 1.15 a.m.
—Alan Wearne

       Kim, I know what's happening; you better know
what's happening. The manager's suspicious and, since he thinks
I know these things, trust me, I say, Kim's mighty clean.
Doesn't he look it? The manager, of course, knows this
but what's, he asks, what's that boy *do*?
                  Can I keep you
out of trouble? What do you think!
                Instead,
I'll circle to my point. In Melbourne
I've this mate, this silly mate. A few weeks back,
whilst I'm down there, Bernie,
who for his sins is something of a poof at times,
Bernie thinks he's met this kid, your age,
who's horny for him. And he is not.
And I was ringside to it: all the set-up,
all the follow-through and final mess, the blubbering threats,
the being mad enough to phone this boy at home,
start to abuse his dad.
           It's okay, this tale hardly fits
my kind of line (and even if it did
I'd never turn on diamond-eyes for you, young Lacy)
but I like what I'm seeing and my point is:
we have to get to know each other better
(isn't that what Bernie's tiny tragedy is
telling us?) much better.
          Yes I know a few Americans:
stand back though, look at your actions, look at them again:
we aren't repeat we aren't in Gangland USA.
And even if we were you're no Al Capone.
Courtesy of Dad you're the local semi-rich kid,
thanks to your few plantations (small, discreet)
trying to make the extra quid, liking the idea
of breaking out.
         But the Americans?
Kim cobber, mate, pal, son, old son,
imagine *them* as a more, much more, ridiculous *us*,
and then imagine *us* trying to play at *them*;
ask: where can, when will, such parodies
cease?
       What the Americans are bringing in
they sure aren't bringing out.
             They're certain to like
what you have and,
though the deal's to swap it for something that,
on occasions, kills (I need to tell you, Kim, kills)
the kids love it.
        I won't even look at it:
me who did my stretch ten/ eleven/ twelve

years back, who coped, but hardly needs to do
much of that again.
                              Could I keep you out of trouble?
Well there's trouble-trouble and there's
getting-caught trouble. What do you think!
All I can advise is Kim, ask yourself:
how far do I wish to travel; and then take your pick.
              Have *I* killed anyone? Have I *killed* anyone? Have I killed *anyone?*
              We should know each other better.
I find it near impossible to reply:
but there may've been this person, so I'll try.
No, I didn't hate this person, probably loved
this person, but one day I returned from where
I'd been to find out what my trust was worth,
what this person truly, quite and simple,
was, had done. Who never knew how caught
they were. Just once I took this person
behind some building (I was being trusted now) and . . .
left them for dead? Let's say
I haven't seen them since.
                              I've killed?
I doubt it.
              Doubts, though, are never enough.
       I hope not.
              You better know what's happening, Kim.

Documentary Poem

THEME:	topical newspaper item
FORM:	block/column style
RHYME SCHEME:	none
METRE:	none
LINE LENGTH:	consistent (right-hand justified)
POEM LENGTH:	maximum 24 lines
TONE:	detached

FORM:
— short lines
— justify both left & right margins to reflect source
— title of article = title of poem
— newspaper name/date below title (smaller font/newspaper name italicised), for example:

Hung Parliament Likely
The Age, August 22, 2010

poem poem poem poem poem
poem poem poem poem poem
poem poem poem poem poem
poem poem poem poem poem

TASK:
— select a newspaper article
— transform dry facts into poetry
— invest poetic imagination & feeling in retelling of story
— bring reportage to life (emotion/imagery/metaphor)
— engage with subject > personify if desired
— create refrain (actual quote from article)
— repeat 2 or 3 times (evolving context)
    "but our football club respects women!"
    "global warming is the New Communism"
    "witnesses reported . . ."
    "a spokeswoman said . . ."
— avoid excessive embellishment
— avoid addition of extra 'facts'
— honour 'the truth'
— exercise in what to *discard* as much as what to *include* (avoid factual overload)
— bring copies of original newspaper article to class...

READING:
— Jordie Albiston 'Sydney Gazette: Address', 'Sydney Gazette: Accidents' *Botany Bay Document*
— Rebecca Edwards 'In the *Armeton Independent* Heart to Heart' *The Road South*
— L.K. Holt 'The Tiger, Ending with a Quote from FOX News' *Keeps*
— Kate Middleton *Ephemeral Waters*
— Richard Tipping 'SOFT RIOTS / TV NEWS' *Penguin Anthology of Australian Poetry*
— Jessica L. Wilkinson 'Bea Lillie to Chaplin' *marionette: a biography of miss marion davies*
— William Carlos Williams *Paterson*

Sydney Gazette: Address
—Jordie Albiston

The first issue of the 'Sydney Gazette and New South Wales Advertiser' appeared in March 1803. The weekly was started by Governor King, and was edited by convict George Howe.

a PAPER in the COLONY
source of solid information   w e
have   courted   assistance   t h e
INGENIOUS and INTELLIGENT
an   exertion   to   merit   t h e
Approbation of the PUBLIC we
open no channel to Political
Discussion   or   Animadversion
we   have   done   our   duty
Innumerable Obstacles we   a r e
happy   to   affirm   were   n o t
insurmountable   the task   before
us   a   liberal   Patronage   to
THE   SYDNEY   GAZETTE
Information our only   Purpose

Sydney Gazette: Accidents
—Jordie Albiston

An inspection on the body of one
Ann   May   wife   of   Lawrence
from   up   Hawkesbury   way
found that contrary to hearsay
he did not murder but she d i d
drink   and died   from her own
excesses.   An infant left   alone
for   less than ten minutes quit
the said spot and was thereafter
absent his mother's mind prey
to   unfavourable   anticipation
called in hopes the little straggler
might hear. On Sunday last a
fire broke out two sacks of
Wheat   were   totally   consumed.
And   upon   the   Wednesday   a
good settler's mare in leaping a
fence   stuck   on   a   pale   by
which   she   immediately   died.

Bea Lillie to Chaplin
—Jessica L. Wilkinson

Bea Lillie to Chaplin: "I suppose any minute now they will all come together and spell out **MARION DAVIES**"

Optical soundtrack of squiggles and bars condensed from many different sounds and sources

THE HOLLYWOOD REVUE OF 1929 and we're singin' in the rain MARIANNE sure I hear you am I blind? Care if I see I'm a bad girl for like you Baby, it's on the level a harmonica ukulele twelve piece band and chorus she is pumping water it's a bonk she takes upon herself a moustache cigar I've got an awful queer feeling and she goes for the fling with her pig in his stomach she's NOT SO DUMB you wish she'd keep on being a nuisance THE FLORADORA GIRL virtually a travesty and engagements always have bad endings—you always finish up *married!* as THE BACHELOR FATHER bubbles over with fun and salted to taste by a tear or two 'cos IT'S A WISE CHILD who tells the exact truth (((or, don't lie any more than you have to he leans on the horn when they kiss—*HONK!* he leans on the horn after saying *Just one more kiss*—*HONK!* I don't want an older woman you suit me exactly after 30 years of age a man is emotionally dead well that's my story and I'm sticking to it until I can think of a better one in FIVE AND TEN you little devil, you made me fall in love with you as the make-up men fix your hair over and give you a mouth and you should look up and say *Do you really? Do you love me?* or get caught on a trip-wire as POLLY OF THE CIRCUS finds her pants and they recite entreat me not to leave thee or to…to…to return from following after thee and blah blah BLONDIE OF THE FOLLIES assuming that there is something to record about the life of a Follies girl and if one accepts this premise we're GOING HOLLYWOOD with Bing! PEG O' MY HEART was a corny story to begin with and a very inferior performance by the star OPERATOR 13, PAGE MISS GLORY without realizing it's HEARTS DIVIDED in an apocryphal script and Dick Powell a Bonaparte cavorting about Baltimore in need of a hair-cut and warbling vacuous ditties about birds and flowers and Paris in the Spring CAIN AND MABEL follows these two losers on the way up and if you don't make the grade you can be a secretary or a sales-girl or any kind of character if you can find it EVER SINCE EVE the ugly duckling throws *The History* out the window as sex takes a holiday—but not for long.

The Tiger, Ending with a Quote from FOX News
—L.K. Holt

Yearly she shrunk, paced; after inexplicable
wait she leapt the 8ft moat and 12ft wall

landing self-cleansed and bristling light
into a strange world of girding shrubbery:

she saw a maladaptive fear of farsight.
At last she saw around the corner

to the kiosk: the music that had terrorised
was nothing, now in view. *Like a broken hedge,*

shall ye be, all the sort of you—The teenage boy,
drunk, taunting, now hanging from

her latch of jaw, was wilder than her,
if wildness be the undeliberated life.

whether the escape was the result of a deliberate act—
police said they've not ruled anything out

Ekphrastic Poem

THEME:	object of choice
FORM:	2 stanzas x 10 lines
RHYME SCHEME:	ababcdedce ('Ode on a Grecian Urn')
METRE:	none

BACKGROUND:
—   'ekphrastic' from Greek *ex* (out) + *phrazein* (explain)
—   ancient form (Homer writing to Achilles' shield in *The Iliad*)

TASK:
—   select photograph/drawing/sculpture/other
—   object should be inanimate
—   bring object to class if possible
—   1st stanza = description
      verbally convey the visual
      be alert to subtlety/detail
      count/measure/weigh/feel/knock/smell/taste
—   2nd stanza = significance
      attempt to *draw out* meaning from object
      extrapolate relationship of concrete thing to self
      render object universal/timeless
      create story

READING:
—   Peter Boyle 'Group Portrait, Delft, late sixteenth century' *New Music*
—   Elizabeth Campbell 'A Mon Seul Desir' *Error*
—   Rosemary Dobson 'The Bystander' *The Road South*
—   Robert Gray 'Ekphrasis' *Coast Road*
—   Paul Hetherington 'Flute in a Museum' *Six Different Windows*
—   A.D. Hope 'On an Engraving by Casserius' *P&W Anthology of Australian Poetry*
—   John Keats 'Ode on a Grecian Urn' *Norton Anthology of Poetry*
—   Kate Middleton 'On a Bronzino in the Uffizi, Florence' *Fire Season*
—   Jan Owen 'Blue Bowl' *Penguin Anthology of Australian Poetry*
—   Peter Porter 'Phar Lap in the Melbourne Museum' *Penguin Anthology of Australian Poetry*
—   Petra White 'Lady's Informal Robe' *A Hunger*

On an Engraving by Casserius
—A.D. Hope

Set on this bubble of dead stone and sand,
Lapped by its frail balloon of lifeless air,
Alone in the inanimate void, they stand,
These clots of thinking molecules who stare
Into the night of nescience and death,
And, whirled about with their terrestrial ball,
Ask of all being its motion and its frame:
This of all human images takes my breath;
Of all the joys in being a man at all,
This folds my spirit in its quickening flame.

Turning the leaves of this majestic book
My thoughts are with those great cosmographers,
Surgeon adventurers who undertook
To probe and chart time's other universe.
This one engraving holds me with its theme:
More than all maps made in that century
Which set true bearings for each cape and star,
De Quiros' vision or Newton's cosmic dream,
This reaches towards the central mystery
Of whence our being draws and what we are.

It came from that great school in Padua:
Casserio and Spiegel made this page.
Vesalius, who designed the *Fabrica*,
There strove, but burned his book at last in rage;
Fallopius by its discipline laid bare
The elements of this Humanity,
Without which none knows that which treats the soul;
Fabricius talked with Galileo there:
Did those rare spirits in their colloquy
Divine in their two skills the single goal?

'One force that moves the atom and the star,'
Says Galileo; 'one basic law beneath
All change!' 'Would light from Achernar
Reveal how embryon forms within its sheath?'
Fabricius asks, and smiles. Talk such as this,
Ranging the bounds of our whole universe,
Could William Harvey once have heard? And once
Hearing, strike out that strange hypothesis,
Which in *De Motu Cordis* twice recurs,
Coupling the heart's impulsion with the sun's?

Did Thomas Browne at Padua, too, in youth
Hear of their talk of universal law
And form that notion of particular truth
Framed to correct a science they foresaw,
That darker science of which he used to speak

In later years and called the Crooked Way
Of Providence? Did *he* foresee perhaps
An age in which all sense of the unique
And singular dissolves, like ours today,
In diagrams, statistics, tables, maps?

Not here! The graver's tool in this design
Aims still to give not general truth alone,
Blue-print of science or data's formal line:
Here in its singularity he has shown
The image of an individual soul;
Bodied in this one woman, he makes us see
The shadow of his anatomical laws.
An artist's vision animates the whole,
Shines through the scientist's detailed scrutiny
And links the person and the abstract cause.

Such were the charts of those who pressed beyond
Vesalius their master, year by year
Tracing each bone, each muscle, every frond
Of nerve until the whole design lay bare.
Thinking of this dissection, I descry
The tiers of faces, their teacher in his place,
The talk at the cadaver carried in:
'A woman—with child!'; I hear the master's dry
Voice as he lifts a scalpel from its case:
'With each new step in science, we begin.'

Who was she? Though they never knew her name,
Dragged from the river, found in some alley at dawn,
This corpse none cared, or dared perhaps, to claim,
The dead child in her belly still unborn,
Might have passed, momentary as a shooting star,
Quenched like the misery of her personal life,
Had not the foremost surgeon of Italy,
Giulio Casserio of Padua,
Bought her for science, questioned her with his knife,
And drawn her for his great *Anatomy*;

Where still in the abundance of her grace,
She stands among the monuments of time
And with a feminine delicacy displays
Her elegant dissection: the sublime
Shaft of her body opens like a flower
Whose petals, folded back expose the womb,
Cord and placenta and the sleeping child,
Like instruments of music in a room
Left when her grieving Orpheus left his tower
Forever, for the desert and the wild.

Naked she waits against a tideless shore,
A sibylline stance, a noble human frame
Such as those old anatomists loved to draw.

She turns her head as though in trouble or shame,
Yet with a dancer's gesture holds the fruit
Plucked, though not tasted, of the Fatal Tree.
Something of the first Eve is in this pose
And something of the second in the mute
Offering of her child in death to be
Love's victim and her flesh its mystic rose.

No figure with wings of fire and back-swept hair
Swoops with his: Blessed among Women!; no sword
Of the spirit cleaves or quickens her; yet there
She too was overshadowed by the Word,
Was chosen, and by her humble gift of death
The lowly and the poor in heart give tongue,
Wisdom puts down the mighty from their seat;
The vile rejoice and rising, hear beneath
Scalpel and forceps, tortured into song,
Her body utter their magnificat.

Four hundred years since first that cry rang out:
Four hundred years, the patient, probing knife
Cut towards its answer—yet we stand in doubt:
Living, we cannot tell the source of life.
Old science, old certainties that lit our way
Shrink to poor guesses, dwindle to a myth.
Today's truths teach us how we were beguiled;
Tomorrow's how blind our vision of today.
The universals we thought to conjure with
Pass: there remain the mother and the child.

Lodestone, lodestar, alike to each new age,
There at the crux of time they stand and scan,
Past every scrutiny of prophet or sage,
Still unguessed prospects in this venture of Man.
To generations, which we leave behind,
They taught a difficult, selfless skill: to show
The mask beyond the mask beyond the mask;
To ours another vista, where the mind
No longer asks for answers, but to know:
What questions are there which we fail to ask?

Who knows, but to the age to come they speak
Words that our own is still unapt to hear:
'These are the limits of all you sought and seek;
More our yet unborn nature cannot bear.
Learn now that all man's intellectual quest
Was but the stirrings of a foetal sleep;
The birth you cannot haste and cannot stay
Nears its appointed time; turn now and rest
Till that new nature ripens, till the deep
Dawns with that unimaginable day.'

Phar Lap in the Melbourne Museum
—Peter Porter

A masterpiece of the taxidermist's art,
Australia's top patrician stares
Gravely ahead at crowded emptiness.
As if alive, the lustre of dead hairs,
Lozenged liquid eyes, black nostrils
Gently flared, otter-satin coat declares
That death cannot visit in this thin perfection.

The democratic hero full of guile,
Noble, handsome, gentle Houyhnhnm
(In both paddock and St Leger difference is
Lost in the welter of money)—to see him win
Men sold farms, rode miles in floods,
Stole money, locked up wives, somehow got in:
First away, he led the field and easily won.

It was his simple excellence to be best.
Tough men owned him, their minds beset
By stakes, bookies' doubles, crooked jocks.
He soon became a byword, public asset,
A horse with a nation's soul upon his back—
Australia's Ark of the Covenant, set
Before the people, perfect, loved like God.

And like God to be betrayed by friends.
Sent to America, he died of poisoned food.
In Australia children cried to hear the news
(This Prince of Orange knew no bad or good).
It was, as people knew, a plot of life:
To live in strength, to excel and die too soon,
So they drained his body and they stuffed his skin.

Twenty years later on Sunday afternoons
You still can't see him for the rubbing crowds.
He shares with Bradman and Ned Kelly some
Of the dirty jokes you still don't say out loud.
It is Australian innocence to love
The naturally excessive and be proud
Of a big-boned chestnut gelding who ran fast.

Lady's Informal Robe
—Petra White

Qing Dynasty, 1890s, National Gallery of Victoria

Paisley, butterflies, grasshoppers, flowers—
and in the robe's red centre, small settled globes
of embroidered trees; threads of a self-contained
world, or a heart nothing ever burst out of.
Staid chair nearby, no-one's to sit on. On the wall
is the portrait of an ugly official whose
dress simply happened to match hers,
the dead so easy to throw together.

The gown shakes itself in the draught, a silk
flapped free of its wearer. Cool as a skin,
it rustles lightness, unbreachable grace:
we'd long to fit it as the foot longed to fit
the tiny slipper, and halved and quartered itself.

Flute in a Museum
—Paul Hetherington

Dragged from dark clay
that had held it fast,
the tune that it sounds
is all aftermath;

all mire and battle
in a ditch near a fort
that the Normans razed
as its bearer fell forward.

Inside the wood
is a trickling stain
like a remnant of breath,
or a song half-played.

Purveyor of charm,
still whole, though rough-hewn,
its music riddles
this upholstered room.

Elegy

THEME:	death of a loved one
FORM:	open/free
RHYME SCHEME:	none
METRE:	none
POEM LENGTH:	maximum 15 lines
STANCE:	1st person singular ("I")

BACKGROUND:
— traditionally an expression of public (rather than private) grief
— poet writes on behalf of society
— lists virtues of deceased
— reflects customs surrounding death specific to culture
— personal/inward grief of poet > Romantic era onwards
— see John Milton's 'Lycidas' > reference point for elegy in English
— see Thomas Gray's 'Elegy Written in a Country Churchyard' > neo-classical elegy
— see Alfred Lord Tennyson's 'In Memoriam' > "in memoriam stanza"

FORM:
— in modern sense, a short poem of ceremonious or formal diction & tone occasioned by death of a person
— differs from dirge, threnody & other forms of pure lament/memorial, but more expansive than epitaph
— no set formal structure

TASK:
— write a short elegy of serious reflection
— focus on small details rather than big event
— tone should be meditative > movement from sorrow toward consolation
— maintain solemn & dignified tone > acceptance
— avoid outpouring of uncontrolled emotion
— contemplate every word & every placement of word
— create a precise tribute impelled by sense of love & loss

READING:
— W.H. Auden 'In Memory of W.B. Yeats' *Seven Centuries*
— Bruce Dawe 'Elegy for Drowned Children' *Penguin Anthology of Australian Poetry*
— Sarah Day 'Wombat' *Grass Notes*
— Robert Gray 'Philip Hodgins' *Coast Road*
— Kris Hemensley "after boy dies" (haiku sequence) *My Life In Theatre*
— Paul Magee 'Elegy' *P&W Anthology of Australian Poetry*
— John Milton 'Lycidas' *Norton Anthology of Poetry*
— Sudesh Mishra 'Elegy: Ee Tiang Hong' *Contemporary Asian Australian Poets*
— Peter Rose 'Ladybird' *Australian Poetry Since 1788*
— Tracy Ryan 'The Argument' *Turnrow Anthology*
— Michael Sharkey 'The Triumph of the Takeaway: A Threnody for John Forbes' *New Music*
— Chris Wallace-Crabbe 'Erstwhile' *P&W Anthology of Australian Poetry*

In Memory of W.B. Yeats
—W.H. Auden

I

He disappeared in the dead of winter:
The brooks were frozen, the airports almost deserted,
And snow disfigured the public statues;
The mercury sank in the mouth of the dying day.
What instruments we have agree
The day of his death was a dark cold day.

Far from his illness
The wolves ran on through the evergreen forests,
The peasant river was untempted by the fashionable quays;
By mourning tongues
The death of the poet was kept from his poems.

But for him it was his last afternoon as himself,
An afternoon of nurses and rumours;
The provinces of his body revolted,
The squares of his mind were empty,
Silence invaded the suburbs,
The current of his feeling failed; he became his admirers.

Now he is scattered among a hundred cities
And wholly given over to unfamiliar affections,
To find his happiness in another kind of wood
And be punished under a foreign code of conscience.
The words of a dead man
Are modified in the guts of the living.

But in the importance and noise of to-morrow
When the brokers are roaring like beasts on the floor of the Bourse,
And the poor have the sufferings to which they are fairly accustomed,
And each in the cell of himself is almost convinced of his freedom,
A few thousand will think of this day
As one thinks of a day when one did something slightly unusual.
What instruments we have agree
The day of his death was a dark cold day.

II

You were silly like us; your gift survived it all:
The parish of rich women, physical decay,
Yourself. Mad Ireland hurt you into poetry.
Now Ireland has her madness and her weather still,
For poetry makes nothing happen: it survives
In the valley of its making where executives
Would never want to tamper, flows on south
From ranches of isolation and the busy griefs,

Raw towns that we believe and die in; it survives,
A way of happening, a mouth.

III

Earth, receive an honoured guest:
William Yeats is laid to rest.
Let the Irish vessel lie
Emptied of its poetry.

In the nightmare of the dark
All the dogs of Europe bark,
And the living nations wait,
Each sequestered in its hate;

Intellectual disgrace
Stares from every human face,
And the seas of pity lie
Locked and frozen in each eye.

Follow, poet, follow right
To the bottom of the night,
With your unconstraining voice
Still persuade us to rejoice;

With the farming of a verse
Make a vineyard of the curse,
Sing of human unsuccess
In a rapture of distress;

In the deserts of the heart
Let the healing fountain start,
In the prison of his days
Teach the free man how to praise.

"after boy dies"
—Kris Hemensley

after boy dies—rain
sudden freeze frames the chaos—
air so clean & sweet

remains thus a week—
after boy dies rain scours yard
of the battle-scene

he was centre of—
oregano resumes shape—
trampled earth perks up—

next day bag windfall
of paramedics' discards—
keep watch where boy died—

speak to him at night
as though angel in a cloud—
leave or stay I say—

no anger or shame—
fly as only the dead fly—
die never again

Found Poem

THEME:	as deemed by found text/s
FORM:	open/free
RHYME SCHEME:	none
METRE:	none
POEM LENGTH:	maximum one page

BACKGROUND:
— found poetry has its roots in Dadaism > appropriation
— method of constructing poems by recycling/repurposing already existing text/s into something new > allopoieses

TASK:
— collect textual fragments from advertising/signage/tickets/labels/graffiti/other
— avoid using literary texts > plagiarism
— seek/detect a unifying sense of theme
— create collage of found text/s
— exploit line turns/caesuras to create 'new' poem
— allow latent energy of found text/s to impel poem
— include 'found poem' in title > indication to reader of appropriation
— NB. spoken (oral) fragments may be used in place of written (textual) fragments

READING:
— Annie Dillard 'Mayakovsky in New York: A Found Poem' *www.poemhunter.com*
— Lisa Gorton 'Graffiti' *Australian Poetry Since 1788*
— Jamie Grant 'The Dictionary Definitions: A Post-modernist Found Poem' *www.poetrylibrary.edu.au*
— Libby Hart 'Overheard conversations—*Parnell Street*' *This Floating World*
— Rudi Krausmann 'Found Poem' *www.poetrylibrary.edu.au*
— Howard Nemerov 'Found Poem' *www.poemhunter.com*
— Hart Seely 'The Unknown' *www.slate.com*
— Richard Tipping 'How Not to Masturbate' *Australian Love Poems*

— view *www.foundpoetryreview.com* & *verbatimpoetry.blogspot.com*

The Dictionary Definitions: A Post-modernist Found Poem
—Jamie Grant

Embodier: one who embodies
Defier: one who defies
Stupefier: one who stupefies
Pacifier: one who pacifies
Speechifier: one who speechifies
Qualifier: one who qualifies
Vilifier: one who vilifies
Nullifier: one who nullifies
Magnifier: one who magnifies
Unifier: one who unifies
      Versifier: one who makes verses

Scarifier: one who scarifies
Purifier: one who purifies
Falsifier: one who falsifies
Ratifier: one who ratifies
Gratifier: one who gratifies
Rectifier: one who rectifies
Sanctifier: one who sanctifies
Stultifier: one who stultifies
Fortifier: one who fortifies
Mortifier: one who mortifies
      Grazier: one who rears cattle

Testifier: one who testifies
Justifier: one who justifies
Satisfier: one who satisfies
Rallier: one who rallies
Replier: one who replies
Multiplier: one who multiplies
Complier: one who complies
Denier: one who denies
Occupier: one who occupies
Crier: one who cries
      Harquebusier: one armed with a harquebus

Decrier: one who decries
Descrier: one who descries
Prier: one who pries
Harrier: one who harries
Worrier: one who worries
Hurrier: one who hurries
Furrier: a dealer in furs
Trier: one who tries
Prophesier: one who prophesies
Envier: one who envies
      Sanguifier: a producer of blood

Found Poem
—Howard Nemerov

after information received in The St. Louis Post-Dispatch, 4 v 86

The population center of the USA
Has shifted to Potosi, in Missouri.

The calculation employed by authorities
In arriving at this dislocation assumes

That the country is a geometric plane,
Perfectly flat, and that every citizen,

Including those in Alaska and Hawaii
And the District of Columbia, weighs the same;

So that, given these simple presuppositions,
The entire bulk and spread of all the people

Should theoretically balance on the point
Of a needle under Potosi in Missouri

Where no one is residing nowadays
But the watchman over an abandoned mine

Whence the company got the lead out and left.
'It gets pretty lonely here,' he says, 'at night.'

How Not to Masturbate
—Richard Tipping

A found poem, taken from Letters to the Editor, *The Sunday Mail*, Adelaide, 26 September 1976.

Art galleries are massage parlours—
don't go in there.
Avoid bushes.
Stay away from Elton John.
Try not to dance.
If you want a good time,
get married.
Otherwise, suffer.

Graffiti
—Lisa Gorton

I wonder this wall can bear the weight of such words
—Graffiti on a wall in Pompeii

The city is smaller than you expected.
Its houses turn their backs on streets—

    And given half a chance
    who wouldn't bunker down behind a stack of silence?
    An arm's length of wall permits any depth of
    meditative calm or your money back—

Its walls are made of potsherds, broken bricks and stone
cut from the hill's mouth, chain-lugged to the city—

    It happened just as you picture it:
    slaves bent double against the weight, whip cracks and flies,
    that crowd in the marketplace breaking off mid-sentence
    to see peace dragged in as a pile of stones—

The stucco of the city walls is everywhere
scratched with these piss-riddled importunities—

    —Cruel Lalagus, why don't you love me?
A wall can bear the weight
    —All the girls love Celadus the Gladiator
The weight is nothing to the wall
    —Caesius faithfully loves M[. . . name lost]
A wall can bear the weight
    —For a good time, turn right at the end of the street.

Out of the dark, ashes fall softly.
We have to stand up again and again to shake them off.
What a weight of light!
The dark is smaller than you expected.

Overheard conversations—*Parnell Street*
—Libby Hart

Would you look at that!
Sweet Jesus.
If it's not one thing, it's another.
Ná bain leis.
You hit the nail on the head.
Unbelievable.
I tell ya.

Ghazal

THEME: love
FORM: closed mono-rhymed couplets
RHYME SCHEME: aA/bA/cA/dA/eA/fA/etc.
METRE: none (in English)
LINE LENGTH: extended
POEM LENGTH: maximum 8 couplets

BACKGROUND:
— ancient Arabic form (C7th)
— canonical by C11th & C12th (Persian/Turkish/Urdu)
— written to rigorously defined Perso-Arabic quantitative metre (untranslatable...)
— classical ghazal limited in theme/vocabulary to earthly/mystical love
— melancholy tone (separation from beloved)
— late western interest > adaptation/modernisation (see Adrienne Rich's sequence)
— translations/modernisation still in progress

FORM:
— couplets
— refrain (*radif*) = small group of words, repeated at end of each second line
— 'a' rhyme (*qafiyah*) appears at head of each refrain, a different word every time
— mention own name toward end of poem (*maqta*) > generally in final line
— each couplet complete unto itself: no enjambment across couplets
— disunity of subject matter a 'unifying' feature . . .
— long lines
— traditional length of poem indeterminate
— couplets should be self-contained, theoretically able to be rearranged
— include 'ghazal' in title

TASK:
— unpack meaning/impact of 'love'
— crystallise/distil 'love' into timelessness
— render the insignificant significant, the daily/domestic universal
— ensure you choose a *qafiyah* which presents sufficient rhyme possibilities!

READING:
— Mirza Ghalib
— John Hollander 'Ghazal on Ghazals' *Rhyme's Reason*
— L.K. Holt 'Bird Ghazal' *Man Wolf Man*
— Gita Mammen 'Ghazal to a Qana Child' *Contemporary Asian Australian Poets*
— Adrienne Rich 'Ghazals: Homage to Ghalib' *The Fact of a Doorframe*
— Philip Salom 'Ghazals on Signs of Love and Occupation' *New and Selected Poems*
— Judith Wright 'The Shadow of Fire: Ghazals' *Phantom Dwelling*
— Jakob Ziguras 'Ghazal' *Australian Love Poems*

Ghazal on Ghazals
—John Hollander

For couplets the ghazal is prime; at the end
Of each one's a refrain like a chime: "at the end".

But in subsequent couplets throughout the whole poem,
It's this second line only will rhyme at the end.

On a string of such strange, unpronounceable fruits,
How fine the familiar old lime at the end!

All our writing is silent, the dance of the hand,
So that what it comes down to's all mime, at the end.

Dust and ashes? How dainty and dry! We decay
To our messy primordial slime at the end.

Two frail arms of your delicate form I pursue,
Inaccessible, vibrant, sublime at the end.

You gathered all manner of flowers all day,
But your hands were most fragrant of thyme, at the end.

There are so many sounds! A poem having one rhyme?
—A good life with a sad, minor crime at the end.

Each new couplet's a different ascent: no great peak
But a low hill quite easy to climb at the end.

Two armed bandits: start out with a great wad of green
Thoughts, but you're left with a dime at the end.

Each assertion's a knot which must shorten, alas,
This long-worded rope of which I'm at the end.

Now Qafia Radif has grown weary, like life,
At the game he's been wasting his time at. THE END.

Haiku

THEME: Australian landscape
FORM: 17 syllables *or less*
POEM LENGTH: 3 lines (5/7/5)
METRE: none
RHYME SCHEME: none
TENSE: perfect present
TITLE: none

BACKGROUND:
— unrhymed Japanese tercet (3-line stanza) recording essence of a moment > immediacy
— originally opening stanza of longer collaborative poem (renga)
— became independent C17th (Basho)
— previously known as *hokku* (until end of C19th)
— subject is natural world/impressionistic > human beings rarely appear
— imagistic/elemental/non-discursive/contemplative/still

FORM:
— comprises 17 *morae* > somewhat awkwardly translated in English as 17 syllables
1 *mora* = 1 short syllable
2 *morae* = 1 long syllable
for example: the word *Nippon* (Japan) = 4 *morae* but only 2 syllables . . .
— written in two semi-independent parts
— parts simultaneously divided & connected by 'cutting' word (*kireji*) to alter mood
— sometimes a caesura (dash/colon/ellipsis) utilised following *kireji*
— *kireji*/caesura occurs at end of first *or* second line
— two parts juxtaposed in terms of image/emotion/thought
— must contain word/phrase indicative of season (*kigo*), for example:
"waratah" = spring
"sleet" = winter
"sunbake" = summer
"crackling leaves" = autumn
NB. over 100 *kigu* per season exist in Japanese . . .

TASK:
— compose five haiku in accepted foreign-adapted 5/7/5 style before bending rules
— attempt to convey Australian landscape (avoid "cherry blossom", etc.)
— avoid articles ("a", "an", "the", etc.)
— select four haiku for class (haiku are traditionally read aloud TWICE)
— avoid writing a weather report!

READING:
— Matsuo Basho
— Bruce Beaver 'Four Hakai' *The Long Game*
— Laurie Duggan 'South Coast Haiku' *Australian Poetry Since 1788*
— Lorin Ford *a wattle seedpod*
— Beverley George *The Birds That Stay*
— Kobayashi Issa
— Andrew Lansdown 'Warrior-Monk' *Australian Poetry Since 1788*

South Coast Haiku
—Laurie Duggan

Rain drips through
the tin roof
missing the stereo

untitled
—Lorin Ford

flooded road
a soft drink bottle
turns left

horseflies!
a wattlebird's welcome
wing snap

untitled
—Beverley George

one tiny feather
all the colours of the bird
weightless on my palm

autumn reflections
the ochre of rockface
warms the river

Imagery Poem

THEME: a performance
FORM: open/free
RHYME SCHEME: optional
METRE: optional
STYLE: descriptive
POEM LENGTH: maximum one page

BACKGROUND:
—   'imagery' akin to 'imitate' > reproduction/simulacrum
—   term dates back to Bible > man made in God's image/graven images

TASK:
—   select a specific performance 'event'
—   write a free form poem from viewpoint of spectator
—   evoke visual display/action by painting (concrete) scene with (abstract) words
—   attempt to convey suspense/thrill/awe of performance
—   avoid mental images > seek energy in the literal . . .

READING:
—   Geoffrey Dutton 'The Beatles in Adelaide' *www.poetrylibrary.edu.au*
—   Anne Elder 'Singers of Renown' *Australian Poetry Since 1788*
—   Alan Gould 'Tightrope Walker' *Australian Poetry Since 1788*
—   Jennifer Harrison 'Hand, Chainsaw and Head' *Australian Poetry Since 1788*
—   Kevin Hart 'The Members of the Orchestra' *Australian Poetry Since 1788*
—   Jan Owen 'Juggler', 'Clown' *Poems 1980–2008*
—   Geoff Page *'Vers libre' Agnostic Skies*
—   Alan Riddell 'At the Hammersmith Palais' *Australian Poetry Since 1788*
—   Patricia Sykes 'living in the palace of the queen of heaven' *Wire Dancing*
—   Richard Wilbur 'Juggler' *www.poemhunter.com*

Vers libre
—Geoff Page

Out on the skateboard
he is writing free verse,
floating up to

rails and benches,
sailing in the lower air.
And it's all just a matter of

muscles and tendons,
of 'going on your nerve',
as Frank O'Hara, New York mystic,

memorably said.
The vocab's in the
knees and ankles,

'ollies', 'kickflips', 'carves' and 'grinds',
the tricks that risk
the full cement,

the moves that sometimes
don't work out—
that bailing to a minor scuttle,

the rolling on a shoulder.
Friends, of course, are part of it
but they are not the point.

The deck, the kerb,
the wheels and he
are writing as the wind might blow

across the options of the concrete
an endless
evanescent poem.

The Members of the Orchestra
—Kevin Hart

Walk onto the dark stage dressed for a funeral
Or a wedding and we, the anxious ones, quieten
As we wait to discover which it will be tonight:

They sit or stand before thin books written
In a foreign script, more alien than Chinese,
But its secret contents will be revealed now

As at the reading of a dead relation's will,
For the last member has entered, slightly late
As befits his honour, like a famous lecturer

With a new theory and a pointer to make it clear.
Alas, he too cannot talk except in the language
Of the deaf and dumb, but as he waves his hands

The members of the orchestra commence their act
Of complicated ventriloquism, each making
His instrument speak our long-forgotten native tongue.

Now one violin speaks above the rest, rehearsing
The articulate sorrow of things in this world
Where we have suddenly woken to find a music

As curious as the relation between an object
And its name. We are taken by the hand and led
Through the old darkness that separates us

From things in themselves, through the soft fold
Of evening that keeps two days apart. And now
Each instrument tells its story in details

That become the whole, the entire forest contained
Within a leaf: the orchestra is quickly building
A city of living air about us where we can live

And know ourselves at last, for we have given up
Our selves, as at our wedding or our funeral,
To take on something new, something that was always there.

Hand, Chainsaw and Head
—Jennifer Harrison

Mortlake Buskers' Festival

He juggles a chainsaw, a rubber hand and plastic head
the ghoulish toys of Quake's dark alphabet—Widow Maker,
Skull Splitter, Brain Biter—old Nordic weapons—their names

too, might find a place in his Mortlake armoury. The day
is sodden, and grey—even the fine patinating rain
feels like sprayed blood on my face and lips. The children

are bored and wish they hadn't come, but when he kick-starts
the chainsaw, they sense the danger of an R-rated thrill.
We're afraid he'll slip and fall on the wet road

but he juggles his macabre salad well, measuring
the saw's jittering arc between eye and wrist, and I admire
the steadiness of his touch as the children become bored even by this.

Returning to Melbourne, they sleep in the back of the car.
The sky falls thick as silk across the windscreen, and over the sound
of wipers and tyres I hear the wind's faint carousing polyphony.

A star drags the ceiling of a cloud. Now and then
houses eulogise the emptiness. The radio crackles and fades
as laden lorries sweep past like mescaline thunder.

The gossip of a child asleep is beautiful, I think,
but where to place ghosts, ghouls and opiate séances—
corpses and the whiskey games of death?

I juggle a machine, the mist and the night—the road thinner
darker than before—danger ahead, out of sight.
Wanting to be entertained, the landscape leans in—watching.

Juggler
—Jan Owen

Tense as a crouching cat, his head thrust out,
canvas heaven above, sawdust underfoot,

in silver tights, a small hole in one thigh,
he sleeks the edge of possibility

with pulsing hands as constant as a heart
and eyes whose darts rehearse a safety net:

flicking his half-smile with a lizard tongue,
he notes the errant orbit, reaches to swing

it into line; and now a dip and turn:
twelve tiers of faces leaning closer in

take up the slack of air, holding their breath
and the edges of their seats, dizzy as faith

that spins in suns and atoms and among
a tarnished juggle of balls in a circus ring

where he has deftly caught the last and bowed.
The centre holds; we sit back reassured.

Imitation Poem

THEME:	community ritual/s
FORM:	long (mimetic) lines
RHYME SCHEME:	none
METRE:	none
POEM LENGTH:	maximum 25 lines
STANCE:	3rd person ("he"/ "she"/ "they")
TENSE:	present

BACKGROUND:
— imitating is how we learn > walking/talking/life drawing

TASK:
— read 'Song Cycle of the Moon-Bone' a number of times (source complete poem if possible)
— digest tone/sentiment/imagery/rhythm/pace
— consider use of nature/symbolism/repetition/punctuation/hyphens/upper-case letters/ellipses/indents/etc.
— examine manner/s in which Murray and Kissane have adapted original
— select one section of song cycle
— imitate style > apply to contemporary communal subject matter
— adhere as closely as possible to impulse/s of original poem
— imitate original title
— NB. exercise only! (close imitation may be considered plagiarism)

READING:
— John Clarke *The Even More Complete Book of Australian Verse*
— Andy Kissane 'The Earlwood-Bardwell Park Song Cycle' *Out to Lunch*
— Les Murray 'The Buladelah-Taree Holiday Song Cycle' *Collected Poems*
— Mary Oliver 'Imitation' (chapter) *A Poetry Handbook*
— Wonguri-Mandjigai People 'Song Cycle of the Moon-Bone' *P&W Anthology of Australian Poetry*

from Song Cycle of the Moon-Bone
—Wonguri-Mandjigai People

1

The people are making a camp of branches in that country at Arnhem Bay:
With the forked stick, the rail for the whole camp, the *Mandjigai* people are making it.
Branches and leaves are about the mouth of the hut: the middle is clear within.
They are thinking of rain, and of storing their clubs in case of a quarrel,
In the country of the Dugong, towards the wide clay pans made by the Moonlight.
Thinking of rain, and of storing the fighting sticks.
They put up the rafters of arm-band-tree wood, put the branches on to
the camp, at Arnhem Bay, in that place of the Dugong . . .
And they block up the back of the hut with branches.
Carefully place the branches, for this is the camp of the Morning-Pigeon man,
And of the Middle-of-the-Camp man; of the Mangrove-Fish man; of two other head-men,
And of the Clay pan man; of the *Baiini*-Anchor man, and of the Arnhem Bay country man;
Of the Whale man and of another head-man; of the Arnhem Bay Creek man;
Of the Scales-of-the-Rock-Cod man; of the Rock Cod man, and of the Place-of-the-Water man.

2

They are sitting about in the camp, among the branches, along the back of the camp:
Sitting along in lines in the camp, there in the shade of the paperbark trees:
Sitting along in a line, like the new white spreading clouds:
In the shade of the paperbarks, they are sitting resting like clouds.
People of the clouds, living there like the mist; like the mist sitting resting with arms on knees,
In here towards the shade, in this Place, in the shadow of paperbarks.
Sitting there in rows, those *Wonguri-Mandjigai* people, paperbarks along like a cloud.
Living on cycad-nut bread; sitting there with white-stained fingers,
Sitting in there resting, those people of the Sandfly clan . . .
Sitting there like mist, at that place of the Dugong . . . and of the Dugong's Entrails . . .
Sitting resting there in the place of the Dugong . . .
In that place of the Moonlight Clay Pans, and at the place of the Dugong . . .
There at that Dugong place they are sitting all along.

3

Wake up from sleeping! Come, we go to see the clay pan, at the place of the Dugong . . .
Walking along, stepping along, straightening up after resting:
Walking along, looking as we go down on to the clay pan.
Looking for lily plants as we go . . . and looking for lily foliage . . .
Circling around, searching towards the middle of the lily leaves to reach the rounded roots.
At that place of the Dugong . . .
At that place of the Dugong's Tail . . .
At that place of the Dugong; looking for food with stalks,
For lily foliage, and for the round-nut roots of the lily plant.

from The Buladelah-Taree Holiday Song Cycle
—Les Murray

1

The people are eating dinner in that country north of Legge's Lake;
behind flywire and venetians. in the dimmed cool, town people eat Lunch.
Plying knives and forks with a peek-in sound, with a tuck-in sound
they are thinking about relatives and inventory, they are talking about customers and visitors.
In the country of memorial iron, on the creek-facing hills there,
they are thinking about bean plants, and rings of tank water, of growing a pumpkin by Christmas;
rolling a cigarette, they say thoughtfully Yes, and their companion nods, considering.
Fresh sheets have been spread and tucked tight, childhood rooms have been seen to,
for this is the season when children return with their children
to the place of Bingham's Ghost, of the Old Timber Wharf, of the Big Flood That Time,
the country of the rationalized farms, of the day-and-night farms, and of the Pitt Street farms,
of the Shire Engineer and many other rumours, of the tractor crankcase furred with chaff,
the places of sitting down near ferns, the snake-fear places, the cattle-cossing-long-ago places.

2

It is the season of the Long Narrow City' it has crossed the Myall, it has entered the North Coast,
that big stunning snake; it has looped through the hills, burning all night there.
Hitching and flying on the downgrades, processionally balancing on the climbs,
it echoes in O'Sullivan's Gap, in the tight coats of the flooded-gum trees;
the tops of palms exclaim at it unmoved, there near Wootton.
Glowing all night behind the hills, with a north-shifting glare, burning behind the hills;
through Coolongolook, through Wang Wauk, across the Wallamba,
the booming tarred pipe of the holiday slows and spurts again; Nabiac chokes in glassy wind,
the forests on Kiwarrak dwindle in cheap light; Tuncurry and Forster swell like cooking oil.
The waiting is buffed, in timber villages off the highway, the waiting is buffeted:
the fumes of fun hanging above ferns; crime flashes in strange windscreens, in the time of the Holiday.
Parasites eave quickly through the long gut that paddocks shine into;
powerful makes surging and pouncing: the police, collecting Revenue.
The heavy gut winds over the Manning, filling northward, digesting the towns, feeding the towns;
they all become the narrow city, they join it;
girls walking close to murder discard, with excitement, their names.
Crossing Australia of the sports, the narrow city, bringing home the children.

3

It is good to come out after driving and walk on bare grass;
walking out, looking all around, relearning that country.
Looking out for snakes, and looking out for rabbits as well;
going into the shade of myrtles to try their cupped climate, swinging by one hand around them,
in that country of the Holiday . . .
stepping behind trees to the dam, as if you had a gun,
to that place of the Wood Duck,
to that place of the Wood Duck's Nest,
proving you can still do it; looking at the duck who hasn't seen you,
the mother duck who'd run Catch Me (broken wing) I'm Fatter (broken wing), having hissed to her children.

from The Earlwood-Bardwell Park Song Cycle
—Andy Kissane

1

The long Holiday is over.
The summer of shorts and bare feet, of sunblock and zinc cream,
of finishing a book and picking up another and finishing it too, is gone.
The summer of the shaded verandah, drinking cold beer
at six o'clock while the children shower, is gone too.
The day of crumpled paper, presents and the big lunch is long gone,
and would not even be a memory but for the bill from Visa waiting
to be paid. The long Holiday is over. The I'm bored Holiday is over.
Vacation Care is done with, its passing loudly celebrated. On this new day
a bodiless CityRail voice apologises for any inconvenience caused.
Cars crawl past school gates like squadrons of worker ants; the children
primped, polished and belted down in the back. They are clean.
There will be just enough time to sneak in a quick kiss
behind the wall of F block, before the Holiday is lined up and forgotten.
The bells rings. It is 9 am.

2

The noise of turbo engines fills the blue sky. High up the blue
is dense and consistent, it needs no air-brushing, no touch up.
But lower down, at the height of roofs and trees, looking to Hurstville
or gazing to the mountains, a hessian-coloured tent of smog
hangs over the suburbs. You can't escape from it.
If you don't happen to notice it this morning—beautiful day,
Jeff says as you buy the Herald—you still have to breathe it in.
It's cars mostly. God Car, as Mundey calls it. The latest monument
to the automobile looms over Turella Park. Architect-designed,
with walls the shade of sandstone, as if it somehow hopes to merge
with the smog. Peregrine falcons circle the stack, a dark blur
against a windowless cliff-face. In the 60s the peregrine
was endangered, absorbing DDT from the rodents and small birds
they ate until they became infertile—laying eggs too soft
to make it. But now their shells are hard again; their young survive.
Like these two falcons who have already breakfasted:
a sudden breath-taking dive too fast for the human eye to follow,
and that was the last the poor mouse knew of life. Now
they are almost at rest, a long leisurely loop over the bush,
before climbing again, cart-wheeling, then tracing the last miles
of the Cooks River as it slithers and slides to the sea.

Journal Poem

THEME: a day in the life...
FORM: sequence poem > dated sections
RHYME SCHEME: none
METRE: none
POEM LENGTH: maximum 2 pages
TONE: intimate

— see SEQUENCE POEM

BACKGROUND:
— Japanese Poetic Diary tradition C10th
— popularised by Beat Poets mid-C20th

FORM:
— traditionally poems interspersed with prose charting travel/daily life

TASK:
— select parts of a prose journal/diary & rewrite as sequence poem
— journal may or may not be previously published, for example:
  The Journals of Captain Cook
  your grandfather's handwritten war memoir
  your own travel diary
— utilise dates/times as subtitles
— attempt to convey sense of time passing > impact on speaker/events
— distil journal entries to their essence
— employ all your poetry skills > do not simply rewrite/break up prose

READING:
— Margaret Atwood *The Journals of Susanna Moodie*
— Emily Ballou *The Darwin Poems*
— Judy Johnson 'From the Journals of Robert Louis Stevenson's Mother' *Nomadic*
— David Lehman *The Daily Mirror*
— Les Murray 'The Scores' *Collected Poems*
— Michael Ondaatje *The Collected Works of Billy the Kid*
— Jan Owen 'Calendar' *Poems 1980–2008*
— Tom Shapcott *Shabbytown Calendar*
— Sei Shonagon *The Pillow Book*

from Calendar
—Jan Owen

after Les Très Riches Heures du Doc de Berry

January   Feasting

'Make January blaze at carrion cold,' I said.
'Be lavish with silver and gold—
plates, tankards, tapestries, and courtiers with gifts.
Approach, I'd have the central figure say—
I, John of Berry, at table in the Great Hall;
and paint yourselves, good sirs, among the crowd.'
There's Hermant swigging down my ale.
Jean flatters me less—pug nose, jowls, wintry smile.
He sees me clear, a skill for which I pay him well.
Why should I, thick-fingered, plain, a practical man,
commission such a work? And at such cost?
(So soon the amaranth robe draws back your gaze!)
As a child I feared my room at night,
those dank grey walls at Vincennes closing in.
Our mother Bonne of Luxembourg would pawn
her jewellery and gowns to pay our debts;
she died of the pestilence when I was nine.
I turned against the dark, the ugliness, the end;
learned my limits: *Le temps viendra*. My choice,
not power like Louis, or learning like Charles,
nor glory like our brother, Philip the Bold.
Pleasure and treasure, I seized on.
But guile and greed serve beauty well,
plunder and bribes can be refined.
Art not alchemy transmutes such gold—
the perfect crafting of this swan and bear,
these endlessly unfolding *Très Riches Heures*.
What will your eyes find to blame or shun
tomorrow in the heavens shimmering here?

February   Fire and Snow

Over the hills, haystacks, and hives,
over the village, wood, and pen,
snow has administered unction,
forgiveness of venial sins.
Precise, austere, it sits in the crook of each tree,
on the upper rush plait of the fence,
clings to the wheel-rim top, thins along the shafts.
There is a grey donkey for humility,
a woodcutter slicing the icy air for diligence,
and the farmer and his wife in the little house,
smocks drawn up, warm cock and quim at the hearth
with the gentle smiles of innocence.

The lady, their mistress, averts her gaze,
raises her blue robe just calf-high,
modesty talking to a cat.
A knot of magpies peck and wait.
The sheep make a sheltered huddle, warm
as the six legs stretched to the flames.

March   Pruning the Vines

A Limbourg brother, the Courtly one,
painted the black fists of the vines
and the winged serpent of gold hovering over
the spire of Lusignan's russet-tiled tower—
a secret form of the fairy Mélusine.
Beyond the oxen lowering their lute horns
and the peasant at the plough, giant-size,
is something new—a darkness over the furrows—
the Master of the Shadows' daring hand,
though by the small crossroads a mountjoy stands
casting no shade. Puzzled you look again—
the soft-muzzled yellow ox is perfectly done
except . . . both right legs forward on its course,
the beast plods onward like a pacing horse.

from **The Scores**
—Les Murray

AUSTRALIA SINCE FEDERATION

1901

When we were all servants
scrubbing off Madam's slurs
I gave up my baby
and the black girl kept hers.
When I got my own high horse
living things felt my spurs
and the flowers were all golden wattle.

1921

That weak word the *Battlers*:
I saw from the train
families punch hoods from wheat bags
to keep out the rain;
Tom said a seller's market
made Australian girls vain
and for Tom the flowers were poppies.

1941

Ar there, Ginger Meggs:
was it Susso tea and suet
put those calipers on your legs?
If Sister Kenny could do it
you'd walk again like a trooper,
left-right and left-right
and the wreaths would be Singapore orchids.

From the Journals of Robert Louis Stevenson's Mother
—Judy Johnson

As for the South Seas . . . I was sick with desire to go there; beautiful places, green for ever; perfect climate, perfect shapes of men and women with red flowers in their hair . . .
—RLS, 1887

June 1888

    Landfall

there is a true hung door in the heart that holds back awe for
fear it should ill place or else overwhelm i never thought to
open it in case all those months at sea might flood through
and i should be washed clear overboard like our unfortunate
camera all the reserve in the world however doesn't prepare
one for certain sights why they call it landfall i cannot imagine
from the deck of the *casco* there rose this heaped swelling nuka
hiva as if a ginger beer plant had fermented all through the
months of our journey and only now was breaking through its
own sheer skin to unveil these cliffs a single eagle etching a
sunned air current with the quill of its wing more
phantasmagorical colours than a seamstress with bundles of
sateen could weep for pearl olive barley sugared bronze that
particular fervid rose a baby blooms in its cheeks when
running the slightest fever it was the heaven and haven louis
dreamed of or so he said as he stood at the railing of our new
life and whispered how hard things would be for him now his
cynicism was gone.

Letter Poem

THEME:	open
FORM:	loose block verse
RHYME SCHEME:	abbab (optional)
METRE:	none
LINE LENGTH:	consistent
POEM LENGTH:	10 lines
STANCE:	1st person singular ("I")

FORM:
— maintain straight right-hand margin (to represent edge of page)
— do not artificially justify
— one 10-line stanza

TASK:
— write a letter in poetic form
— keep lyrical
— letter should *imply* without disclosing all facts, because correspondents already know
    one another *or* content sets scene by default
— open with "Dear"/"My"/"To Whom It May Concern"/other
— close with "From"/"Yours"/"Best Wishes"/other
— suggestions:
    lover to beloved
    soldier to mother
    adopted child searching for biological roots
    pen pal
    Letter to the Editor
    Dear John letter
    office memo
    chain letter
    letter to Santa Claus
    summons

READING:
— Elizabeth Bishop 'Letter to N.Y.' *The Complete Poems*
— Leonard Cohen 'Famous Blue Raincoat' *Concise Leonard Cohen*
— Brook Emery 'Dear K, it's light that makes the river flow' *Collusion*
— Brook Emery 'Postscript: like Picasso' *P&W Anthology of Australian Poetry*
— Jan Owen 'The Letter' *Poems 1980–2008*
— Marcella Polain 'postcards from spain' *New Music*
— Wendy Poussard 'Telegram from Grandmother' *Family Ties*
— Elizabeth Riddell 'The Letter' *P&W Anthology of Australian Poetry*
— Jennifer Strauss 'A Mother's Day Letter: Not for Posting' *Family Ties*

Letter to N.Y.
—Elizabeth Bishop

FOR LOUISE CRANE

In your next letter I wish you'd say
where you are going and what you are doing;
how are the plays, and after the plays
what other pleasures you're pursuing:

taking cabs in the middle of the night,
driving as if to save your soul
where the road goes round and round the park
and the meter glares like a moral owl,

and the trees look so queer and green
standing alone in big black caves
and suddenly you're in a different place
where everything seems to happen in waves,

and most of the jokes you just can't catch,
like dirty words rubbed off a slate,
and the songs are loud but somehow dim
and it gets so terribly late,

and coming out of the brownstone house
to the gray sidewalk, the watered street,
one side of the buildings rises with the sun
like a glistening field of wheat.

—Wheat, not oats, dear. I'm afraid
if it's wheat it's none of your sowing,
nevertheless I'd like to know
what you are doing and where you are going.

The Letter
—Elizabeth Riddell

I take my pen in hand
            there was a meadow
beside a field of oats, beside a wood,
beside a road, beside a day spread out
green at the edges, yellow at the heart.
The dust lifted a little, a finger's breadth;
the word of the wood pigeon travelled slow,
slow half pace behind the tick of time.

To tell you I am well and thinking of you
and of the walk through the meadow, and of another walk

along the neat piled ruin of the town
under a pale heaven empty of all but death
and rain beginning. The river ran beside.

It has been a long time since I wrote. I have no news.
I put my head between my hands and hope
my heart will choke me. I put out my hand
to touch you and touch air. I turn to sleep
and find a nightmare, hollowness and fear.

And by the way, I have had no letter now
For eight weeks, it must be
a long eight weeks
because you have nothing to say, nothing at all,
not even to record your emptiness
or guess what's to become of you, without love.

I know that you have cares
ashes to shovel, broken glass to mend
and many a cloth to patch before the sunset.

Write to me soon and tell me how you are
if you still tremble, sweat and glower, still stretch
a hand for me at dusk, play me the tune,
show me the leaves and towers, the lamb, the rose.

Because I always wish to hear of you
and feel my heart swell and the blood run out
at the ungraceful syllable of your name
said through the scent of stocks, the little snore of fire,
the shoreless waves of symphony, the murmuring night.

I will end this letter now. I am yours with love.
Always with love, with love.

postcards from spain
—Marcella Polain

i hold your postcards careful as a pack of lies
& i see that you are living amongst ponderous exteriors
that yearly   miles of wall erupt with scarlet bougainvillea
i am learning the geography of flowers
& you teach me   like a bird mother
that plazas can be orange groves with
wide & tangerine umbrellas sprouting prehistoric between trees
that dense purple flowers fringe your buildings
like an outsized tablecloth
that valley drops like gasp
like god stepped there & all the earth just rushed away
& that   on every side   cliffs retain this

utter as a fingerprint
clear as the image of your face   that light
minute by minute   certain & invisible
deepens like a mouth

in answer to your questions:
i am looking for you everywhere
studying the handstitched shape of each rosette
it takes to make a skirt for small & dark-eyed girls
the dusty slant of donkey rump
the strands of faded braid laid there
the face of a boy told to sit
to turn this way
or that
for me
your hungry chick
open-mouthed
to kiss

Postscript: like Picasso
—Brook Emery

A man's just sitting there on the crescent
taking it all in or letting it all pass by,
the traffic, birdcall, the sun that falls
on his bald head polishing it like Picasso's,
all brown and round and shining,
sitting there like a stone or a frog or a Buddha.

He is of it all, even this speeding past,
the wheels that push away contradictions
between the need to grip and the need to
slip away. He must feel the cars pull air after them
in packets, swoosh, swoosh, and another
swoosh, as he sits there in the gaps, persistently.

List Poem

THEME:	open
FORM:	open/free, with list element
RHYME SCHEME:	optional
METRE:	none
POEM LENGTH:	maximum 2 pages
TENSE:	present

FORM:
— poem is composed using list as unifying device
— anaphoric structure (word/phrase repetition) may also evoke sense of list

TASK:
— compose a list of items relating to chosen theme
— choose a mixture of significant & (apparently) insignificant items
— think about ways in which items may interrelate > concatenation
— remain as detached as possible > let items do the work . . .
— concentrate on meaningful ways to open & close poem
— allow list elements to create mesmerising effect > litany
— ensure poem 'goes' somewhere . . .

READING:
— Kevin Brophy 'What I believe' *P&W Anthology of Australian Poetry*
— Barbara Giles 'Learning all the Words in the World' *P&W Anthology of Australian Poetry*
— Nazim Hikmet 'Things I Didn't Know I Loved' *100 Great Poems of the Twentieth Century*
— Bronwyn Lea 'Why I Write' *Australian Poetry Since 1788*
— Frank O'Hara 'To the Film Industry in Crisis' *100 Great Poems of the Twentieth Century*
— Gig Ryan 'If I Had A Gun' *New and Selected Poems*
— John A. Scott 'My Favourite Things' *Penguin Anthology of Australian Poetry*
— Ouyang Yu 'An Identity CV' *Contemporary Asian Australian Poets*

If I Had A Gun
—Gig Ryan

I'd shoot the man who pulled up slowly in his hot car this morning
I'd shoot the man who whistled from his balcony
I'd shoot the man with things dangling over his creepy chest
in the park when I was contemplating the universe
I'd shoot the man who can't look me in the eye
who stares at my boobs when we're talking
who rips me off in the milk-bar and smiles his wet purple smile
who comments on my clothes. I'm not a fucking painting
that needs to be told what it looks like.
who tells me where to put my hands, who wrenches me into position
like a meccano-set, who drags you round like a war
I'd shoot the man who couldn't live without me
I'd shoot the man who thinks it's his turn to be pretty
flashing his skin passively like something I've got
to step into, the man who says *John's a chemistry PhD*
and an ace cricketer, Jane's got rotten legs
who thinks I'm wearing perfume for him
who says *Baby you can really drive* like it's so complicated,
male, his fucking highway, who says *ah but you're like that*
and pats you on the head, who kisses you at the party because
everybody does it, who shoves it up like a nail
I'd shoot the man who can't look after himself
who comes to me for wisdom
who's witty with his mates about heavy things
that wouldn't interest you, who keeps a little time
to be human and tells me, female, his ridiculous
private thoughts. Who sits up in his moderate bed
and says *Was that good* like a menu
who hangs onto you sloppy and thick as a carpet
I'd shoot the man last night who said *Smile honey*
don't look so glum with money swearing from his jacket
and a 3-course meal he prods lazily
who tells me his problems: his girlfriend, his mother,
his wife, his daughter, his sister, his lover
because women will listen to that sort of rubbish
Women are full of compassion and have soft soggy hearts
you can throw up in and no-one'll notice
and they won't complain. I'd shoot the man
who thinks he can look like an excavation-site
but you can't, who thinks what you look like's for him
to appraise, to sit back, to talk his intelligent way.
I've got eyes in my fucking head. who thinks if he's smart
he'll get it in. I'd shoot the man who said
Andrew's dedicated and works hard, Julia's ruthlessly ambitious
who says *I'll introduce you to the ones who know*
with their inert alcoholic eyes
that'll get by, sad, savage, and civilized
who say *you can* like there's a law against it
I'd shoot the man who goes stupid

in his puny abstract how-could-I-refuse-she-needed-me
taking her tatty head in his neutral arms like a pope
I'd shoot the man who pulled up at the lights
who rolled his face articulate as an asylum
and revved the engine, who says *you're paranoid*
with his educated born-to-it calm
who's standing there wasted as a rifle
and explains the world to me. I'd shoot the man who says
Relax honey come and kiss my valium-mouth blue.

Learning all the Words in the World
—Barbara Giles

Walking accomplished, so much energy
goes into words. Each object named
with glee, each name a part of object,
each object recollectable by name
for her admiring listeners.

She sits on the edge of conversation,
practising. 'Shattered', she says, and 'Tipsy',
'Wild goose chase', 'Naïve'. The talkers
glance at her and stop their talk of rape,
rummaging in memory for paradigms
of infant apperception. One recalls
fear, of a gaggle of geese, the other, blame,
defiance, ashes in the mouth.

They cease to scold, sweetening their words, but soon
they're back to what's more natural to them,
rapping the world from pot to politics.
The child turns pages carefully, intoning,
'Apple: fish: jaguar: peacock: unicorn'.
Studious, prim, 'Nuclear war', she says.

What I believe
—Kevin Brophy

I believe the world is round like a ball and spins through space.
This belief helps me get along with neighbours and work colleagues.
Without it I would be mad or sick, I believe.
I believe there are human footprints on the moon.
This belief helps me to bear watching television news.
I believe that money is the shadow of infinity,
that I will die and know nothing about it.
I believe you are like me.

92

This belief, I believe, makes me a fool or an optimist.
I believe most of us mistake the present for the past,
and that the future is the past;
that what is right is nearly always obvious;
that belief works best as a necessity or a distraction.
I believe the universe is a dangerous place.
I believe that God is an elaborate and mediocre idea;
that panic is our companion,
and travelling through space will be the last of our tasks.
I believe the purpose of all this is the creation of memory.
I believe most beliefs are yet to be discovered.
I believe in what is most fragile and uncertain,
the paragraph, for instance, or clouds; rain; leaves.
I believe death makes love possible,
and that if you do not train them at once your beliefs
        will bark all night.

Why I Write
—Bronwyn Lea

Because up the coal road way the bees came out so nicely.
Because I have got my rifle cleaned out and she is bright as a whistle.
Because the geese are in and one of them lays.
Because it rained very heavily and some of the road washed away.
Because every jack one of our cows have got calves.
Because the baby is crying. Tiara is sewing. Ellee is propping her face up.
Because Dad and Mr Jackson got the maul and struck Jerry just above the nose.
Because when I am older I want to drive a twenty ton articulated tip truck.
Because do you know who it was? Well, it was Ben Price!
Because I get wild in a second.
Because Uncle and Dad and Uncle Charlie went out egging in the Mary.
Because Alfred Douglas has had 50 cuts with the cane.
Because I have had the cane once and stood on the form twice.
Because Fairy is a bit lame on her nearside foreleg. She had a stone in it.
Because they had the inquest in the new dinner room.
Because Lall said she won't be good friends with Carrie.
Because I am learning music.
Because Don says the orange trees will bear fruit in seven years.
Because I wish you many happy returns.
Because the bees came out so nicely and began to clean their home.

Love Poem

THEME:	romantic love
FORM:	open/free
RHYME SCHEME:	optional
METRE:	optional
STANCE:	1st/2nd person ("I"/ "you")
TONE:	intimate
POEM LENGTH:	maximum one page

BACKGROUND:
—   romantic love is one of the oldest poetic themes
—   love poems exist across all languages/cultures
—   good love poems are difficult to write > everything has been said before . . .

TASK:
—   compose a poem addressed to your lover/husband/wife
       or
       compose a poem to celebrate the wedding of two friends > 'epithalamium'
—   consider new love, forbidden love, enduring love, late love, love at first sight
—   concentrate on small, seemingly insignificant details > synecdoche encouraged
—   frame details within larger rubric of grand love
—   avoid cliché/hyperbole > focus on understatement
—   maintain stable, personal tone > quiet celebration

READING:
—   Andrew Carruthers 'Love's Legend, a Sermon' *Contemporary Asian Australian Poets*
—   Michael Farrell 'The Ménage' *Australian Love Poems*
—   Andy Jackson 'Millstones and Wings' *Australian Love Poems*
—   Jill Jones 'The Night Before Your Return' *Macquarie PEN Anthology*
—   James McAuley 'Celebration of Love' *P&W Anthology of Australian Poetry*
—   Michael Sharkey 'untitled' *Australian Love Poems*
—   Edmund Spenser 'Epithalamion' *Norton Anthology of Poetry*
—   Ken Taylor 'Epithalamium' *New Music*
—   Mona Van Duyn 'Late Loving' *Poets Laureate Anthology*

untitled
—Michael Sharkey

That you contain the world: the quartet
for the end of time, the seven last words,
and the Cross, the Buddha's mind,
the Prophet's head, the earth that breathes,

the sky that falls in children's tales,
the tide that ebbs, the moon's Swiss cheese,
Nijinsky's dance, Stravinsky's *Flood*;
what if I said you're all of these:

a Gadda plot, a Dowland song,
an awful mess, a Dior dress,
a Zegna suit, a pigeon shoot,

a botched translation from a dream,
a Bach transcription for a lute—
not one assertion would be wrong.

Epithalamium
—Ken Taylor

All I give you this day
comes apart in my hands
and breaks,
as this wave breaks
on hidden slopes of sand
and stone
and spreads in skeins of foam
to be lost forever.

But I shall be constant
as the waves
and this gift of my heart
will form and form again beside you
and say
as the surf says to the shore:
I make you,
you make me.
It will always be thus.

Memory Poem

THEME: natural disaster
FORM: 3 short sections
RHYME SCHEME: none
METRE: none
POEM LENGTH: approximately 20 lines
STANCE: 1st person singular ("I")

—   see SEQUENCE POEM

FORM:
—   1st section = exposition > beginning "I remember . . ."
        clear, decisive description
        place yourself at event site
—   2nd section = denial > beginning "I don't remember . . ."
        sense of repression (what you don't *want* to remember)
        sense of irony (remembering what is *not* remembered)
—   3rd section = climax > beginning "I will never forget . . ."
        convey power of subconscious to intrude into conscious thought
        aspects of event etched into memory forever
—   separate sections with asterisks, numerals, subtitles, other

TASK:
—   select a catastrophe occurring in the natural world, for example:
        bushfire
        flood
        cyclone
        earthquake
        avalanche
        climate change
—   research/particularise
—   access mental images as though actual recollections
—   endeavour to bring event to life by exploring emotional effects/aftermath
—   allow small/peculiar details to tell story
—   catastrophe may be treated as metaphor for inner human state

READING:
—   Jordie Albiston 'Three Memoirs' *Botany Bay Document*
—   Luke Davies 'North Coast Bushfires' *Penguin Anthology of Australian Poetry*
—   Martin Harrison 'Remembering Floodwater' *Australian Poetry Since 1788*
—   Susan Hawthorne *Earth's Breath*
—   W. Flexmore Hudson 'Drought' *Penguin Anthology of Australian Poetry*
—   John Jenkins 'Push This Wall Back' *P&W Anthology of Australian Poetry*
—   Ted Kooser *The Blizzard Voices*
—   David Musgrave 'Tsunami', 'Postcards from a Drought' *Phantom Limb*

Postcards from a Drought
—David Musgrave

1.
A pair of exercise bikes
parked on a concrete slab
in the front yard of the house
in the middle of the harrowed plain.

2.
Bore water lashing
the grass and the daisies,
a green iris
in a bloodshot eye.

3.
Umbrella grass lost
in the corners of sheds,
piled high to the ceilings:
an ossuary of fine, spoked bones.

4.
A busy highway
beginning somewhere out back
ends at the biscuit jar,
jammed with ants.

5.
A bust of Voltaire
smiles too much
in a dusty sunroom
stacked with leather suitcases.

6.
Wood pigeons and wasps
drink from the covered bathtub.
Lowing warily, starved of grass,
cattle graze the lawn.

7.
Bowsers of oats, water,
petrol. From the road,
fine dust storms leap
over them and vanish.

8.
Eight linked maidens
dance around the outside
of a stained cement urn. Frogs
inside it croak like prophets.

9.
Making love in the afternoon,
trying for a child; almost at random
white butterflies flower
over coarse lawn.

10.
Venus wakes us up at 3am
intruding among the trees
and then ascending,
dwindling.

11.
On the fourth day of Christmas
crows rise
from pepper trees
staining the grid, the dust.

12.
A dead tree quivering:
a bird springs into
a bush. And then resumes
its funerary.

13.
Cyclone wire. A blue-tongued
lizard garrotted attempting
a rhomboid. A storm
of ants at its head. Clear sky.

14.
Wires have disappeared
from the telegraph poles.
Everything goes underground
in this heat.

15.
Sundial in shadow,
spare clouds drift.
Buried at its base,
grandparents' ashes.

16.
An ancient woman forgets
the name of her daughter-in-law.
Wet ice slips
in an empty wine glass.

17.
In the distance cars hover
on liquid haze
and sink
into the dry road.

North Coast Bushfires
—Luke Davies

Reverence. How the afternoon
comes down on you like that.
In a microsleep you can travel
hundreds of metres—into trees
and cars. I thought I would
just close my eyes. After that
it is all pretty random.
The universal joint, the bearing pins.

So I tried to focus on clouds.
They billowed just like anvils.
I smelled smoke long before the cops
closed off the highway.
On backroads the sunlight slanted
through dust and I pictured the roll
of the earth. The sky turned orange.
But everyone had the same idea.

At dusk a black soot filled
the valley where a lone tree stood.
It was like driving through fog, only
it burnt the throat. Then lightning
lit that tree which said, 'I have
grown into a god.' And stray thoughts
were telling me how badly I needed
a motel. Because life is long.

Metaphor Poem

THEME: animal world
FORM: open/free
RHYME SCHEME: none
LINE LENGTH: varied
POEM LENGTH: approximately 18 lines

BACKGROUND:
—   free form poetry traced to roots of lyric
—   non-metrical structure
—   heavy reliance on grammatical breaks
—   absence of regular end-rhyme
—   isolated phrasing
—   variable line length/poem length
—   deliberate breaking off/headlong continuity
—   unpredictability

FORM:
—   'metaphor' = figure of speech, from Greek (to carry from one place to another)
     "in a black hole" (depressed, not in a real hole)
     "eyes glued to the tv" (watching closely, not actually stuck)
     "spinning a yarn" (telling a story, not twirling a thread)
     "keeping it under his hat" (keeping a secret, nothing to do with a hat)
     "getting her hands dirty" (doing the difficult part of a task)
     "cold comfort" (appears to be reassuring, but actually not)
     "not my cup of tea" (don't like it)
     "be a devil" (take a chance)
     "hit the mark" (achieve an objective)

TASK:
—   select specific creature (insect/reptile/fish/bird/mammal)
—   observe & reflect
—   take notes re relevant/identifying characteristics
—   research objectively (dictionary/atlas/internet/documentary/gardening guide)
     NB. you are collecting technical information at this stage, not gathering lines
—   put research notes away for day or two
—   consider chosen creature anew
—   construct free form poem using animal as metaphor for an inner human state >
     pathetic fallacy
—   keep metaphor consistent & clean > avoid catachresis

READING:
—   Judith Beveridge 'The Shark' *Storm and Honey*
—   Judith Bishop 'Rabbit' *Penguin Anthology of Australian Poetry*
—   Elizabeth Campbell 'Structure of the Horse's Eye' *Australian Poetry Since 1788*
—   Rebecca Edwards 'Draw a Lion' *P&W Anthology of Australian Poetry*
—   Robert Gray 'Flying Foxes' *Coast Road*
—   Sarah Holland-Batt 'Winter Harmonica' *P&W Anthology of Australian Poetry*
—   John Kinsella 'Goat' *Australian Poetry Since 1788*
—   Anthony Lawrence 'Sooty Oystercatchers, Venus Tusk Fish' *New & Selected Poems*
—   Mark Tredinnick 'Catching Fire; or, the Art of Sitting' *Turnrow Anthology*

Structure of the Horse's Eye
—Elizabeth Campbell

Under the sun, the horse's eye
is a glass dome over a petal, the pupil a raised bud
of pollinated velvet, bisected;

the horizon in it. Almost 360—
a narrow corridor behind
and one spot in front of her nose, are blind.

Curious about the wolf? Find a fat horse
grazing at dozey noon her home paddock;
try to creep up.

In the waking night her eyes are flat opals
bouncing your torch as you pan the black
like a river for green-gold flakes,

or better; go sightless to hear
the known rhythm coming out the dark.
Within, the *tapetum*, mirrorlike, reflects all

available light back through her retina—
Homo sapiens, one of few mammals
lacking this useful aid, to nocturne,

mostly sleeps. *Equus* watches on her feet.
Sometimes a night visit sets them off—
swilling around you like surf in a tide pool

pushing the long bones
of their heads at you. The honest creature
investigates with her face, magnolia

nostrils cupping the scent
of palms up empty at arms length. Your image
shone back on the convex surface of the eye-pool

is macrocephalic, duck-billed, your skull
a helpless baby too heavy for itself.
If you want to better love the world,

ask counsel of those who never come inside;
her order, *perissodactyla*
(large mammals with odd numbered toes)

have largely failed. Taxonomy
progresses, dividing its names. Sometimes a life,
pressing on, proves its point

but Life does not. Let her advance—
she is herself, through flowering heads; eyes careful,
thinking nothing of advancement,

above lips tough enough to strip
the exquisite thistle-crown from its armoured stem.
How excellent is her tail! She draws all grass

through the bone-set strata of her teeth,
grazing 12 hours in her open-lidded present—
deep time made one dimension

by limited depth perception, wide world
made pasture and shelter. Let her head's long neck
lift to her clear-edged ear

whose hearing threads in darkness the Earth
to its sky. Let her steady herbivorous day
blink open and consume and close it all.

The Shark
—Judith Beveridge

We heard the creaking clutch of the crank
as they drew it up by cable and wheel
and hung it sleek as a hull from the roof.

Grennan jammed open the great jaws
and we saw how the upper jaw hung from
the skull. We flinched at the stench of blood

that dripped on the fishhouse floor, and
even Davey—when Grennan reached in
past the scowl and the steel prop for the

stump—just about passed out. The limb's
skin had already blanched, a sight none
of us could stomach, and we retched—

though Grennan, cool, began cutting off
the flesh in knots, slashing off the flesh
in strips; and then Davey, flensing and

flanching, opened up the stomach and
the steaming bowels. Gulls circled like
ghouls. Still they taunt us with their cries

and our hearts still burn inside us when
we remember, how Grennan, with a tool,
took out what was left of the child.

Goat
—John Kinsella

Goat gone feral comes in where the fence is open
comes in and makes hay and nips the tree seedlings
and climbs the granite and bleats, through its line-
through-the-bubble-of-a-spirit-level eyes it tracks
our progress and bleats again. Its Boer heritage
is scripted in its brown head, floppy basset-hound ears,
and wind-tunnelled horns, curved back for swiftness.
Boer goats merged prosaically into the feral population
to increase carcass quality. To make wild meat. Purity
cult of culling made vastly more profitable. It's a narrative.
Goat has one hoof missing—just a stump where it kicks
and scratches its chin, back left leg hobbling, counter-
balanced on rocks. Clots of hair hang like extra legs
off its flanks. It is beast to those who'd make devil
out of it, conjure it as Pan in the frolicking growth
of the rural, an easer of their psyches when drink
and blood flow in their mouths. To us, it is *Goat*
who deserves to live and its "wanton destruction"
the ranger cites as reason for shooting on sight
looks laughable as new houses go up, as dozers
push through the bush, as goats in their pens
bred for fibre and milk and meat nibble forage
down to the roots. Goat can live and we *don't know*
its whereabouts. It can live outside nationalist tropes.
Its hobble is powerful as it mounts the outcrop
and peers down the hill. Pathetic not to know
that it thinks as hard as we do, that it can loathe
and empathize. Goat tells me so. I am being literal.
It speaks to me and I am learning to hear it speak.
It knows where to find water when there's no water
to be found—it has learned to read the land
in its own lifetime and will breed and pass its learning
on and on if it can. Goat comes down and watches
us over its shoulder, shits on the wall of the rainwater
tank—our lifeline—and hobbles off
to where it prays, where it makes art.

Metrical Poem

THEME: illness
FORM: 2 sestets
METRE: personal choice
RHYME SCHEME: optional

BACKGROUND:
— 'metre' from Greek *metron* (measure) > metronome
— metric unit = poetic foot
— (regularly recurring metric units are not utilised in free form poetry...)

FORM:
— there are six main metric units (feet) in poetry:
    (1)   iamb: re<u>mote</u> / de<u>cide</u> / de<u>lay</u> / de<u>feat</u> / a<u>new</u> / be<u>cause</u> / for<u>get</u>
    (2)   trochee: <u>Tues</u>day / <u>fath</u>er / <u>an</u>swer / <u>walk</u>ing / <u>sea</u>son / <u>fore</u>ign
    (3)   anapaest: interr<u>upt</u> / reconn<u>ect</u> / inter<u>vene</u> / Portug<u>uese</u> / Gali<u>lee</u>
    (4)   dactyl: <u>po</u>etry / <u>Sat</u>urday / <u>al</u>ien / <u>suff</u>ering / <u>beau</u>tiful / <u>cel</u>ebrate
    (5)   spondee > two short stressed syllables: north-west / outside / downtown
    (6)   pyrrhic > two short unstressed syllables: it is / when the / if you
— scansion = metrical analysis of a poem
    symbol used to denote (stressed) beat/pulse/accent = ′
    symbol used to denote (unstressed) offbeat = ˘
— metre is created by systematic/regular use of one main metric unit per line:
    3 x unit = trimeter
    4 x unit = tetrameter
    5 x unit = pentameter
    6 x unit = hexameter
    7 x unit = heptameter
— while a variety of units may be utilised in a metrical poem, one will dominate, thus categorising that poem as belonging to a particular metre

TASK:
— focus on an illness/disease/malfunction of body or mind
— compose two 6-line stanzas using a metrical line of your choice, for example:
anapaestic trimeter > 'Twas the <u>night</u> before <u>Christ</u>mas, when <u>all</u> through the <u>house</u> (Clement Clarke Moore)
trochaic tetrameter > <u>By</u> the <u>shores</u> of <u>Gitche</u> <u>Gum</u>ee (Henry Wadsworth Longfellow)
iambic pentameter > And <u>fill</u> all <u>fruit</u> with <u>ripe</u>ness <u>to</u> the <u>core</u> (John Keats)
— establish & maintain regularity of pulse
— attempt to create a 'natural music' consistent from beginning to end

READING:
— Anne M. Carson 'On the ebb-tide' *Removing the Kimono*
— Bruce Dawe 'Doctor to Patient' *P&W Anthology of Australian Poetry*
— John Donne 'A Hymne to God the Father' (iambic pentameter) *Seven Centuries*
— Jennifer Harrison 'Chemotherapy' *Australian Poetry Since 1788*
— Gwen Harwood 'The Night Watch' *Bone Scan*
— John Leonard 'Rhythm, Form and Metre' (essay) *Seven Centuries*
— C.C. Moore 'A Visit from St. Nicholas' (anapaestic trimeter) *www.poetryfoundation.org*
— Sylvia Plath 'Fever 103' *Ariel*

A Visit from St. Nicholas
—Clement Clarke Moore

'Twas the night before Christmas, when all through the house
Not a creature was stirring, not even a mouse;
The stockings were hung by the chimney with care,
In hopes that St. Nicholas soon would be there;
The children were nestled all snug in their beds;
While visions of sugar-plums danced in their heads;
And mamma in her 'kerchief, and I in my cap,
Had just settled our brains for a long winter's nap,
When out on the lawn there arose such a clatter,
I sprang from my bed to see what was the matter.
Away to the window I flew like a flash,
Tore open the shutters and threw up the sash.
The moon on the breast of the new-fallen snow,
Gave a lustre of midday to objects below,
When what to my wondering eyes did appear,
But a miniature sleigh and eight tiny rein-deer,
With a little old driver so lively and quick,
I knew in a moment he must be St. Nick.
More rapid than eagles his coursers they came,
And he whistled, and shouted, and called them by name:
"Now, *Dasher!* now, *Dancer!* now *Prancer* and *Vixen!*
On, *Comet!* on, *Cupid!* on, *Donder* and *Blixen!*
To the top of the porch! to the top of the wall!
Now dash away! dash away! dash away all!"
As leaves that before the wild hurricane fly,
When they meet with an obstacle, mount to the sky;
So up to the housetop the coursers they flew
With the sleigh full of toys, and St. Nicholas too—
And then, in a twinkling, I heard on the roof
The prancing and pawing of each little hoof.
As I drew in my head, and was turning around,
Down the chimney St. Nicholas came with a bound.
He was dressed all in fur, from his head to his foot,
And his clothes were all tarnished with ashes and soot;
A bundle of toys he had flung on his back,
And he looked like a pedler just opening his pack.
His eyes—how they twinkled! his dimples, how merry!
His cheeks were like roses, his nose like a cherry!
His droll little mouth was drawn up like a bow,
And the beard on his chin was as white as the snow;
The stump of a pipe he held tight in his teeth,
And the smoke, it encircled his head like a wreath;
He had a broad face and a little round belly
That shook when he laughed, like a bowl full of jelly.
He was chubby and plump, a right jolly old elf,
And I laughed when I saw him, in spite of myself;
A wink of his eye and a twist of his head
Soon gave me to know I had nothing to dread;
He spoke not a word, but went straight to his work,

And filled all the stockings; then turned with a jerk,
And laying his finger aside of his nose,
And giving a nod, up the chimney he rose;
He sprang to his sleigh, to his team gave a whistle,
And away they all flew like the down of a thistle.
But I heard him exclaim, ere he drove out of sight—
"Happy Christmas to all, and to all a good night!"

A Hymne to God the Father
—John Donne

Wilt thou forgive that sinne where I begunne,
    Which is my sin, though it were done before?
Wilt thou forgive those sinnes through which I runne,
    And do them still: though still I do deplore?
        When thou hast done, thou hast not done,
            For, I have more.

Wilt thou forgive that sinne by which I wonne
    Others to sinne? and, made my sinne their doore?
Wilt thou forgive that sinne which I did shunne
    A yeare, or two: but wallowd in, a score?
        When thou hast done, thou hast not done,
            For I have more.

I have a sinne of feare, that when I'have spunne
    My last thred, I shall perish on the shore;
Sweare by thy selfe, that at my death thy Sunne
    Shall shine as it shines now, and heretofore;
        And, having done that, Thou haste done,
            I have no more.

Doctor to Patient
—Bruce Dawe

Please sit down. I'm afraid I have some
rather bad news for you: you are now seventeen
and you have contracted an occupational disease called
unemployment. Like others similarly afflicted
you will experience feelings of
shock, disbelief, injustice, guilt, apathy, and aggression
(although not necessarily in that order)
and you'll no doubt be urged to try the various
recommended anodynes: editorials in newspapers,
voluntary unpaid work for local charities, booze,
other compulsive mind-destroyers, prayer, comforting
talks with increasingly less-interested friends.
106

It is small comfort to know that the disease
is universal and can accommodate
the middle-aged and thirtyish and strikes down
those in camps in Kompong Sam and Warsaw.
However you will discover, as time passes,
that your presence in itself will make others
obviously uncomfortable. Try not to let
your shadow, at this stage,
fall across your neighbour's plate; eat
with the right hand only; do not touch
others in public (this can be easily
misconstrued); keep always
down-wind, if possible. Please remember
you have now become our common vulnerability
personified. Oh yes, and, by the way,
you will be relieved to know the disease
is only in a minority of cases terminal.

Most, that is, survive. Next, please.

Chemotherapy
—Jennifer Harrison

The man I see daily
in the hospital gym, is nobody's father.
He strains beneath the barbell
but doesn't forget the small observation
sheltering between his thighs.
He drags his body back and forth
pumping sero-positive blood
out from his heart into his muscle
and back to his heart
in a silent daily circuit
a smooth oiling of sweat
a machine fear won't quit with.
He throws caution aside
and looks in the mirror, seeing thinness.
He wipes away chalk from his hands
while I continue laps in the 25-metre pool
pushing my arms through water
the temperature of warm blood.
His bald head is a twin moon to mine.
I feel for him, as for a brother
the intimacy of the sick.
We need not speak to know the task.
We exercise away our particular knowledge
mine of motherless children
and his of a death
sewn into quilts the size of football fields.

Monochord

THEME: longing
FORM: one line
METRE: none

—   see VILLANELLE

FORM:
—   one line of self-contained poetic writing
—   whole poem condensed to one line *or* fragment of abandoned poem
—   not necessarily full sentence
       simple statement
       straight description
       snippet of dialogue
       emotional reaction
       evocation of sense (sight/smell/etc.)

TASK:
—   write a minimum of ten monochords
       five ending 'a' rhyme (for example: "ing")
       five ending 'b' rhyme (for example: "all" / "le")
       (these monochords will be utilised in VILLANELLE exercise)

READING:
—   John Anderson *The Shadow's Keep*
—   Claire Gaskin 'thirty-six aphorisms and ten-second love stories' *Paperweight*
—   Ian McBryde *Slivers*
—   Yannis Ritsos *Monochords*
—   Chris Wallace-Crabbe 'The Poem of One Line' *Turnrow Anthology*

from *Monochords*
—Yannis Ritsos

11.   Oxygen-welders, oxygen-welders, the lanterns on trains—

26.   Glory, a rock, in spite of its wings.

117.   Are we complete, then, only in emptiness?

267.   I'd like to say something Greek, and make it dawn.

286.   How quietly time collapses into poetry.

from *The Shadow's Keep*
—John Anderson

the everywhere the moon always was and rests

maintain the ruins of the previous restoration

strange and erudite sobs and passions

Why stage an Aristotle of significance?

cold sonnets share my name

from thirty-six aphorisms and ten-second love stories
—Claire Gaskin

2.   Remaining retained because it is eccentric to do so.

14.   I found the tragedy to match my temperament.

17.   What value do you place on your love relegations.

34.   In torch light you replaced my windscreen wipers.

35.   You have kept a maidenhair alive for thirty years.

Monologue

THEME:	emotional state/s
FORM:	couplets
RHYME SCHEME:	internal assonance/alliteration
METRE:	none
STANCE:	1st person (lyric "I")
POEM LENGTH:	24 lines

BACKGROUND:
— ancient dramatic technique > 'subjective posture'
— includes prayer/lament/much lyric verse
— form perfected in Victorian era

FORM:
— a monologue is *spoken*
— a monologue is spoken *alone*
— verbal 'utterance' (as opposed to written word)
— similar to soliloquy > uninterrupted speech
— speaker is not 'the poet'
— clear connection to drama > *implied audience* (no speaker speaks in complete isolation . . .)
— audience may be external (addressed as such) *or* internalised (self-revelation/ meditation)
— monologue actually heard *or* (often) overheard . . .
— emphasises subjective/personal aspect of speech
— may be single voice representing unitary view point

TASK:
— compose poem in 2-line stanzas
— adopt persona (or mask)
— conceive situation (avoid overly dramatic . . .)
— present varying emotions of single mind
— verbalise inner thoughts, consciously or distractedly > Othello/Hamlet
— convey temperament/character of speaker
— attempt to reveal tension between 'poet' & 'speaker' of poem (see Sylvia Plath's poem)
— mull over situation aloud

READING:
— Robert Browning 'My Last Duchess' *Norton Anthology of Poetry*
— John Jenkins 'Six O'clock Swill' *P&W Anthology of Australian Poetry*
— Emma Lew 'They Flew Me in on the Concorde from Paris' *Australian Poetry Since 1788*
— Sylvia Plath 'Lady Lazarus' *Norton Anthology of Poetry*
— Philip Salom 'The Composer Shostakovich Orders His Funeral' *P&W Anthology of Australian Poetry*
— William Wordsworth 'Lines Composed a Few Miles Above Tintern Abbey' *Seven Centuries*

from Lines Composed a Few Miles Above Tintern Abbey
—William Wordsworth

Five years have past; five summers, with the length
Of five long winters! and again I hear
These waters, rolling from their mountain-springs
With a soft inland murmur.—Once again
Do I behold these steep and lofty cliffs,
That on a wild secluded scene impress
Thoughts of more deep seclusion; and connect
The landscape with the quiet of the sky.
The day is come when I again repose
Here, under this dark sycamore, and view
These plots of cottage-ground, these orchard-tufts,
Which at this season, with their unripe fruits,
Are clad in one green hue, and lose themselves
'Mid groves and copses. Once again I see
These hedge-rows, hardly hedge-rows, little lines
Of sportive wood run wild: these pastoral farms,
Green to the very door; and wreaths of smoke
Sent up, in silence, from among the trees!
With some uncertain notice, as might seem
Of vagrant dwellers in the houseless woods,
Or of some Hermit's cave, where by his fire
The Hermit sits alone.

The Composer Shostakovich Orders His Funeral
—Philip Salom

What is *Negativity*? What is *Sarcasm*?
If it's anything like 100 proof, I'll drink it.
It patters in my stomach like a snare drum,
yes: the tense skin (psoriasis) the drumstick
allegros which clatter down the wrist.
The minor keys always, the only big beats
(savage) of Stalin's Boots, his banging
up the staircase at 4am (bedwetting time).
Got your little suitcase packed? *Composer?*

My music could end with a single
note: a hole in the back of the neck.
I hear thousands of notes, a symphony
and nothing happens. He grunts once,
and thousands die. Who moves more people?
Who is the Greatest Artist? Composer Stalin!

What kind of citizen does he want?!
The Future: a one-size-for-all blow-up doll,
eyes wide open, legs wide open, mouth shut.

Yes, opinions nil. A clean arse.
Paranoia turned out into the snow sets cold.
Don't say anything wrong, or your son
will denounce you. Ah, yes, he has.

The West burnt their red-hot brand
on me, their man who fell from the rack
into detractions, denunciations, post mortems.
What's *A Soviet Artist's Reply to Just Criticism*?
Why is the mighty Ninth, the Beethovean
Romantic Knee-Trembler instead a Knee-Jerk
Dud? Either that or dedicate it in Glory
to the Secretary General Himself—do
my best work for Him? I shit instead.

The Great Puppeteer Himself! Little
Shostakovich is just a click-jointed player
chewing his lips . . . ventriloquism for manic
mixed metaphors: Tragedy is everywhere but
look, listen: everyone is happy, happy,
oh, everyone is well informed, or well
-informed on. Unhappiness is not allowed.

Arh, accused yet again: damned and damned
from Stalin down, from US academics up.
In the West they know everything—that the puppet
is the real me. In the West they just don't kill
their artists like they used to. We do.
Arthur Miller is rightly shaken seeing me.
I am a native of Shaken.
                           Even the Age's Seer
after a night of coffee and heavy dossiers
needs an outlet: what a noise he makes
pissing into the water of the toilet.
There! That's Greatness. *That's* music.
Uh uh, too much gravity . . .
General Tractor Anthemist! Blight of Agriculture.
Piss in the snow. Piss in the faces of the damned.
Why won't somebody kill him?

Andante, adagio, standstill.
The window panes are sheets of vodka
but I get sober looking through them.
When I go walking I breathe out
from my note-perfect memory
clouds of absence: poets, peasants, generals,
all killed equally. Is life any easier
because of music? I need a coat and scarf:
I hear silenced gunshots in the snow.

Old women he broke, Party men who
shat their pants every day they met him,
fall down in despair. He is dead. *Dead?*

00 proof. Bastard.
Ah Nikita: and the thaw, the freeze, thaw, freeze.
Ah Brezhnev, grey suits, bleak and buttons,
a frieze of medals. I could hang a whole sonata
in the space between his nose and his lips.

I think I'll die.

They Flew Me in on the Concorde from Paris
—Emma Lew

They flew me in on the Concorde from Paris.
We were fortunate not to burn.
Over Shanghai I observed to my flautist husband,
"Such a metropolis needs a decent opera house."
He rejected me in late May.
I resolved in future to express my feelings through my garden,
With an archway of zucchinis and cucumbers,
A bed of apothecary roses and high-yield grass seeds.

In the carpark at the Institute of Space Research
Women workers were performing their role of holding up half the sky,
While shipping companies complained about reserves of grain
Silting up the anchorage and all the sputnik could do was bleep.

I lodged with a senior government official in four elegant pavilions
Named after four seasons and bedecked with imitation sheep carcasses.
It was almost unthinkable not to give,
But I had no hard currency and could not afford contraceptives.
Thus I took a tonic in winter to be able to hunt tiger in spring.

I delivered my acceptance speech in the Great Hall of the People.
Citing the Scripture of Mountains and Seas,
I began by calling on steel makers to take up the way of Lamaism.
"Let's start calming down!" I cried.
"Let's get off painting and onto banking.
Differences are secondary to common interests,
They should not affect bilateral ties in a larger sense."

I was applauded by reformists and conservatives alike.
Tell that to the lady in the morgue.
And tell her,
"When you get to heaven,
Maybe you'll get some answers."

Myth Poem

THEME: Classical Greek myth
FORM: open/free
RHYME SCHEME: none
METRE: none
POEM LENGTH: maximum 18 lines

BACKGROUND:
—   ancient Greek myths have retained relevance for many reasons:
     Oedipal Complex
     Elektra Complex
     narcissism
     atlas
     Atlantic Ocean
     company logos > Pegasus/phoenix/trident
     the Olympics
     Disney (Pluto/Bambi)
     art (Picasso's 'Vollard Suite' > minotaur/Botticelli's 'Birth of Venus')
     film ('Troy'/'Fantasia')
     books ('Narnia' / 'Harry Potter')
     classical music (Gustav Holst's 'The Planets'/Richard Strauss' 'Elektra')
     solar system > planets/star constellations
     space mission Apollo
     Nike running shoes (winged goddess of victory)
     Venus > goddess of love > venereal disease
     the 'Midas touch'
     Mars Bar
     Ajax cleanser (Greek warrior who 'cleaned up' in Trojan war/s)
     cars (Saturn/Aurora/Orion/etc.)
     periodic table (Mercury/Titanium/Hydrogen/Uranium/etc.)
     Amazon online bookstore

TASK:
—   select an ancient Greek myth that appeals to you
—   consider relevance of myth to contemporary life
—   adapt accordingly > imagery/language/events
—   compose modern myth poem, retaining essence of original (names, basic plot)
—   allow form to reflect motion/momentum of story
—   bring myth alive > context/dialogue/symbolism/thought processes

READING:
—   Diane Fahey 'Andromeda' *P&W Anthology of Australian Poetry*
—   Paul Hetherington 'A Contemporary Icarus' *Six Different Windows*
—   Dorothy Hewett 'Psyche's Husband' *Penguin Anthology of Australian Poetry*
—   Evan Jones 'Eurydice Remembered' *P&W Anthology of Australian Poetry*
—   Katheryn Lomer 'Everyday Ophelia' *Motherlode*
—   Kate Middleton 'Penelope on the Night of Odysseus' Homecoming' *Fire Season*
—   Adrienne Rich 'Orion' *Norton Anthology of Poetry*
—   Gig Ryan 'Electra to Orestes' *New and Selected Poems*
—   Alex Skovron 'Sisyphus' *Sleeve Notes*

Everyday Ophelia
—Kathryn Lomer

In deep bathwater I am Ophelia, mad from love,
but I have one ear on a Janet Frame mnemonic—
Read Over Your Greek Book In Verse—the other
cocked to baby squeals. A quarter-tone shift,
delight to distress, and I leap, leaving water trails
like a puzzle, to bring him in. He jerks his beaky mouth
over my breasts like a grazing Galapagos turtle,
alights on a morsel and hangs, resting an ear on my heart.
We are any mammals, the southern right whale and calf
glimpsed from a glider cliff in a moment like this one,
rare as whooping cranes, generous as sunshine.
You are a sleight of hand, conjured from a paper hat,
a living fossil of an ancient love. Only you are innocent.
We count hours now, not days.
There is no plan and there are no new dreams.
I could lower blinds, curl up and scorn the light
but you are just beginning to shape a world.
You need every good thing and I must give it.
So we lie under oak leaf patterns, watching wind,
counting waves, remembering birdsong.
A bank of cloud lumbers in from the north
threatening to take the shine from autumn's equinox,
rain thieved last week from the Timor Sea
holding its breath above us, a meniscus,
fragile airborne tension waiting to break.
One cloud hangs like a zeppelin,
a trick of afternoon light turning its side to a rainbow.
Read over your Greek book in verse, I say,
and you laugh as if it's the best thing
you've heard in all your life.

Andromeda
—Diane Fahey

She was the first pin-up.
Naked and bejewelled
she was chained to a rock
then thrown by heavy-breathing
winds into wild postures:
at each new angle, lightning
popped like a photographer's flash.

The gold circling her neck
matched her hair, the emeralds
her eyes, the rubies her nipples,
and the amethysts those bruises.

In lulls of wind, she pulled
against iron, stood almost straight.
The sky was a mouth swallowing her,
the sun a glimmering eye.
Lolling in the tide, a sea-dragon
slithered and gurgled like
some vast collective slob.

From afar, Perseus saw her first
as a creature writhing on a rock;
close-up, she was a whirlpool
of rage and terror and shame.
The dragon he changed to stone
with hardly a thought.
But his strength almost failed him
in breaking those chains.

Looking away from her nakedness
he smooths her ankles, wrists.
She waits for the moment
when he will meet her eyes.

Sisyphus
—Alex Skovron

I choose my boulders carefully,
They are scattered like words across the white plain;
I scoop my syntax from the cloud's dictionary—
The path to wisdom is difficult, rich and mundane.
I have my nostalgia, the soft exquisite aching
That lulls and lacerates; and I can dream
The dazzling city that drives upward to the horizon
Beyond the land where the rumbling boulders lean.
One evening soon, as the crescent overtakes me,
I'll slip discreetly over the edge of the plain
And into the valley beyond, because I know
The song of terrible grace that summons me.
But the clouds are backing away; an exquisite pain
Is pleading for me to stay. How can I go?

Electra to Orestes
—Gig Ryan

(to a friend, leaving)

My friend, before we met I was in pain
as one who loved me I could not requite
and so pretended for some paltry gain
of status, satire, end to cabled night,
to return affection when faith had shone
its last extinguished prick—then this was made—
faithless sand he built an edifice on
and I colluded, mired in false trade.
Then recognition blasted into wit
to apprehend what I had thought had died
for true love souvenirs and now unfit
to love, but now you prove me wrong who ride
the ceaseless world, not injured but inured
to former life. How have I since endured?

Penelope on the Night of Odysseus' Homecoming
—Kate Middleton

for Julian Novitz

There is a rumour of a golden realm,
an ocean both pacific and terribly blue
and we keep company with the magician, chance—
the whispering alchemist. In Greek
the lapping waves of the Black Sea mouth the word
kindly, kindly—as, kindly, we fall into
and out of each other, become bound
and unbound.

All beds have their secrets, lover.
All beds hold
the artful mesh of sleep and sleeplessness.

It will be two thousand years from now until man
discovers any new planet, and until then
nightly we will meet here—the auditors
of all quenchable desires.

Ode

THEME:	tribute to a person
FORM:	3 sections
RHYME SCHEME:	optional
METRE:	none
TONE:	positive
STANCE:	2nd person ("you")
POEM LENGTH:	maximum one page

—   see SEQUENCE POEM

BACKGROUND:
—   'ode' from Greek *odein* (to chant)
—   classical antiquity > Sapphic ode, Pindaric ode, Horatian ode
—   ceremonial/heroic tribute to elevate leader/athlete/etc., often impelled by exaggerated adulation/flattery > 3 sections (strophe, antistrophe, epode)
—   revitalised by Romantic poets > lyric ode (philosophical reflection on nature/ art/the soul)
—   'tribute' = an act/statement/gift intended to show gratitude/respect/admiration

FORM:
—   write a poem in three sections tributing a particular person
—   separate sections with asterisk/numeral/other
—   person may be intimate acquaintance or public figure
     parent
     sibling
     child
     friend/workmate
     or
     political/religious leader
     quiet achiever
     firefighter
     sportsperson
     artist
—   each section to represent new thought/timeframe/angle/etc.

TASK:
—   use poem as vehicle to express all you would like to say (or would like to have said) to person in question ...
—   address person > tribute is *direct* . . .

READING:
—   Bruce Beaver 'Ode XIII' *Penguin Anthology of Australian Poetry*
—   John Forbes 'Death: An Ode' *Penguin Anthology of Australian Poetry*
—   Thomas Gray 'Ode' *Norton Anthology of Poetry*
—   Gwen Harwood 'An Impromptu for Ann Jennings' *P&W Anthology of Australian Poetry*
—   John Keats 'To Autumn' *John Keats: The Complete Poems*
—   Allen Tate 'Ode to the Confederate Dead' *Poets Laureate Anthology*
—   Petra White 'Ode to Coleridge' *A Hunger*

Ode
—Thomas Gray

ON THE DEATH OF A FAVORITE CAT,
DROWNED IN A TUB OF GOLDFISHES

'Twas on a lofty vase's side,
Where China's gayest art had dyed
     The azure flowers that blow;
Demurest of the tabby kind,
The pensive Selima, reclined,
     Gazed on the lake below.

Her conscious tail her joy declared;
The fair round face, the snowy beard,
     The velvet of her paws,
Her coat, that with the tortoise vies,
Her ears of jet, and emerald eyes,
     She saw; and purred applause.

Still had she gazed: but 'midst the tide
Two angel forms were seen to glide,
     The genii of the stream:
Their scaly armor's Tyrian hue
Through richest purple to the view
     Betrayed a golden gleam.

The hapless nymph with wonder saw:
A whisker first and then a claw,
     With many an ardent wish,
She stretched in vain to reach the prize.
What female heart can gold despise?
     What cat's averse to fish?

Presumptuous maid! with looks intent
Again she stretched, again she bent,
     Nor knew the gulf between.
(Malignant Fate sat by and smiled)
The slippery verge her feet beguiled,
     She tumbled headlong in.

Eight times emerging from the flood
She mewed to every watery god,
     Some speedy aid to send.
No dolphin came, no Nereid stirred;
Nor cruel Tom, nor Susan heard;
     A favorite has no friend!

From hence, ye beauties, undeceived,
Know, one false step is ne'er retrieved,
      And be with caution bold.
Not all that tempts your wandering eyes
And heedless hearts, is lawful prize;
      Nor all that glisters, gold.

To Autumn
—John Keats

I
Season of mists and mellow fruitfulness,
      Close bosom-friend of the maturing sun;
Conspiring with him how to load and bless
      With fruit the vines that round the thatch-eaves run;
To bend with apples the mossed cottage-trees,
      And fill all fruit with ripeness to the core;
          To swell the gourd, and plump the hazel shells
      With a sweet kernel; to set budding more,
And still more, later flowers for the bees,
Until they think warm days will never cease,
          For Summer hast o'er-brimmed their clammy cells.

II
Who hath not seen thee oft amid thy store?
      Sometimes whoever seeks abroad may find
Thee sitting careless on a granary floor,
      Thy hair soft-lifted by the winnowing wind;
Or on a half-reaped furrow sound asleep,
      Drowsed with the fume of poppies, while thy hook
          Spares the next swath and all its twinéd flowers:
And sometimes like a gleaner thou dost keep
      Steady thy laden head across a brook;
      Or by a cider-press, with patient look,
          Thou watchest the last oozings hours by hours.

III
Where are the songs of Spring? Aye, where are they?
      Think not of them, thou hast thy music too—
While barréd clouds bloom the soft-dying day,
      And touch the stubble-plains with rosy hue;
Then in a wailful choir the small gnats mourn
      Among the river sallows, borne aloft
          Or sinking as the light wind lives or dies;
And full-grown lambs loud bleat from hilly bourn;
      Hedge crickets sing; and now with treble soft
      The redbreast whistles from a garden-croft;
          And gathering swallows twitter in the skies.

Death: An Ode
—John Forbes

Death, you're more successful than America,
even if we don't choose to join you, we do.
I've just become aware of this conscription
where no one's marble doesn't come up;
no use carving your name on a tree, exchanging vows
or not treading on the cracks for luck
where there's no statistical anomalies at all
& you know not the day nor the hour, or even if you do
timor mortis conturbat me. No doubt we'd
think this in a plunging jet & the black box recorder
would note each individual, unavailing scream
but what gets me is how compulsory it is—
'he never was a joiner' they wrote on his tomb.
At least bingeing becomes heroic & I can see
why the Victorians
so loved drawn-out death-bed scenes:
huddled before our beautiful century, they knew
what first night nerves were all about.

One-Sentence Poem

THEME:	a walk
FORM:	block
RHYME SCHEME:	none
METRE:	none
POEM LENGTH:	maximum 14 lines
STANCE:	2nd person ("you")

BACKGROUND:
A semicolon (;) separates parts of a sentence that need a stronger break than a comma, but not as strong a break as a period. It is used to join two complete sentences that are closely related.
"The past was a different time; they did things differently then."
"A man chooses; a slave obeys."

A colon (:) is used instead of a period at the end of a sentence, to indicate that something else is to follow (which is NOT a complete sentence in itself).
"Buy these things: milk, bread, popcorn."
"There are lots of items on sale: a real temptation . . ."

Dashes & parentheses are used around extra information not essential to the sentence.
"It is difficult to cope with too many tasks—two or three are sufficient—without getting a headache..."
"It will not be easy to prove that the man is guilty (as some may say) of stealing."

Of course, a sentence may employ all these devices at once.
"He was confused about the directions she (quickly) wrote out, & then gave—sealed in an envelope—to him; he was unsure where to go: right or left, or down the hill: through the town, or back around the lake."

—   NB. hyphens are *short* dashes used to join two words > "right-handed"

TASK:
—   construct a poem comprising one extended (punctuated) sentence
—   attempt to sustain one grammatical sentence over many lines
—   exercise in control, effective line-breaks, precision punctuation
—   convey sense of long, uninterrupted walk
—   employ full spectrum of punctuation (if required) in order to facilitate meaning
—   take care to exploit full use of line-breaks

READING:
—   Dan Disney 'on locating the essence of the dinner party' *and then when the*
—   Toby Fitch 'Orbits' *Rawshock*
—   Robert Gray 'Description of a Walk' *Coast Road*
—   Emma Jones 'Conversation' *Australian Poetry Since 1788*
—   John Keats 'Bright Star' *Seven Centuries*
—   Geoff Page 'The Sentence' *Agnostic Skies*
—   Theodore Roethke 'Big Wind' *Norton Anthology of Poetry*
—   Alex Skovron 'Full Moon, Thebes' *Towards the Equator*

Bright Star
—John Keats

Bright star, would I were stedfast as thou art—
    Not in lone splendor hung aloft the night
And watching, with eternal lids apart,
    Like nature's patient, sleepless Eremite,
The moving waters at their priestlike task
    Of pure ablution round earth's human shores,
Or gazing on the new soft-fallen mask
    Of snow upon the mountains and the moors;
No—yet still stedfast, still unchangeable,
    Pillow'd upon my fair love's ripening breast,
To feel for ever its soft swell and fall,
    Awake for ever in a sweet unrest,
Still, still to hear her tender-taken breath,
And so live ever—or else swoon to death.

The Sentence
—Geoff Page

For some years now
he's wanted to write
a sentence *à la* Henry James,

a sentence of some length, *mais oui,*
with several subtle
subordinate clauses

and certain sly parentheses,
inserted as required,
a sentence that will share the weather

and, on its way, be light with thought,
a tone detached but
dense with gossip,

a sound that says: Surrender now
this precious fortnight of your life,
I have a story here for you—

and stories must be never hurried—
and, yes, most probably it has
Americans, fresh-faced in Europe

back before the First World War,
consorting with *La Belle Époque,*
or something rather like it,
where money's rarely any problem

and you, dear reader, in due course,
will find you've somehow come to care

for these sweet mannequins of mine
who, starting from a well-made phrase,
can stroll for days in sentences

as sinuous as air.

Conversation
—Emma Jones

"Oh this and that. But for various reasons"—
(the season, and the change in season, the season of grief

and retrospection, the rooftop pulled from the childhood
house, and the internal doll in its stuck seat,

that is, the fictive soul in its brute cathedral, and because of memory,
maybe, and organs in niches, and the beat to things,

and the knowledge that the body is the soul and vice versa,
but that false distinctions are sometimes meaningful,

and that difference, all difference, is just distance, not a state,
not a nation, and because nothing *matters*, not really,

or everything does, I don't mind being an animal, at all,
because a sentient thing is nothing else, and because toward matter

I feel neither love nor hate but the kind of shuttered Swiss
neutrality a watch might feel for time

if it had an animal's sentiments, knowing itself a symbol
and function, knowing itself a tool, and because I feel

the dull culmination of various phenomena informing me
and am that culmination, I feel ill in some small way,

though not ill really, just idle, and I prefer, you see,
to keep an impassive inviolable pact with things that tick,

with solitary, shifted things, and because my life's approximate act
is the sister to some other life, with different tints, I carry

and nurse, my diffident twin, I'm often morose, and think
of those statues that lean above themselves in water,

those fountains, stone, with commemorative light,
with disfiguring winds, and because reflection is an end in itself

124

and because there's an end even to reflection, and an end to the eye,
that heated room, I prefer to keep my artifice and my arsenal

suspended, close; like an angled man; like the stationed sun;
and because matter ends, or I should say, matter turns to matter,

and my small inalienable witness to this is real, I can't pretend
to wish to be a rooted thing, full-grown, concerned

with practical matters, in a rooted world, and careful of borders,
when an ineradicable small portion glints, my mind, that alma mater,

and says, make your work your vicarage)—"I put off going back".

Orbits
—Toby Fitch

(after a line by Prévert)

This money that rolls
that doesn't stop rolling,
stock market blackouts
and bigwigs purring, cars inter-
secting, generations over
-lapping, bungled-up bank accounts
from slow-colliding satellites,
a break-up in static, snowballs in the air-
waves as a world
-wide tide nibbles away
at coastlines,
gulping little souls on lunch-
break, running from an overheated
greenhouse into the red,
run into the ground by imps,
their spastic euros, dispensed
from plastic trees, fluctuating in the air
-con, impulsively combusting in record time,
please sign on the dotted line ...

while outside, an unmanned unicycle drifts by

and all the gulls,
even the ones that aren't hungry,
fly upside down and in circles, green-
backed by green spotlights
that hypnotize the blank-cheque sky.

Pantoum

THEME:	the body
FORM:	cross-rhymed quatrains with repeated lines
RHYME SCHEME:	abab/bcbc/cdcd/etc.
METRE:	none
POEM LENGTH:	maximum 8 quatrains

BACKGROUND:
—   C15th Malayan origin > *pantun*
—   reached English via France (Victor Hugo/Baudelaire)
—   constructed in 4-line stanzas
—   pantoums are of indeterminate (any) length
—   tight mesmerising chain of echoes
—   unexpectedly hypnotic repetitions
—   anti-narrative form, perfect for evoking the past (4 steps forward, 2 steps back)
—   static/wooden at worst, strange/wonderful at best
—   American poets sometimes add final hanging line (not recommended)

FORM:
—   each quatrain rhymes abab
—   unspecified length of poem (generally 5 or 6 stanzas)
—   lines 2 & 4 of first quatrain become lines 1 & 3 of next quatrain, & so on
—   final quatrain uses lines 3 & 1 from first stanza as lines 2 & 4, thus completing circle
—   a 5-stanza pantoum is formatted thus:

1st stanza	1, 2, 3, 4
2nd stanza	5(2), 6, 7(4), 8
3rd stanza	9(6), 10, 11(8), 12
4th stanza	13(10), 14, 15(12), 16
final stanza	17(14), 18(3), 19(16), 20(1)

TASK:
—   compose a pantoum celebrating/exploring part/s of the human body
—   repeated lines may be extended/manipulated (with restraint)
—   enjambment permitted, in order to refresh form
—   body may be treated as metaphor for inner human state

READING:
—   John Anderson 'Strange and Erudite Sobs and Passions' *The Shadow's Keep*
—   Grant Caldwell 'a short history of the future' *glass clouds*
—   John Forbes 'Four Heads & how to do them' *P&W Anthology of Australian Poetry*
—   Stephen Fry 'The Pantoum' *The Ode Less Travelled*
—   Claire Gaskin 'in her hands' *a bud*
—   Jane Gibian 'Parts of the tongue' *P&W Anthology of Australian Poetry*
—   Alan Gould 'Port of Melbourne Song' *The Past Completes Me*
—   Emma Lew 'Detail for a Lily Scheme' *Australian Poetry Since 1788*
—   Kate Llewellyn 'Breasts' *Penguin Anthology of Australian Poetry*
—   David Musgrave 'Phantom Limb' *Phantom Limb*

a short history of the future
—Grant Caldwell

in uncertain glass you
wake and wake to
the history tapes
in nests of space

you wake and wake
to eyes of loss and longing
in nests of space
strange in their appearance

these eyes of loss and longing
you can't concede
how strange is their appearance
in spite of their commotion

you can't concede
as long as the stars
in spite of the commotion
rise above the morning

as long as the stars
in the singing space of scars
rise above the morning
immense as atoms

in the singing space of scars
your mind sails on
immense as atoms
in the illusion of such stillness

your mind sails on
each moment stacked
in the illusion of such stillness
like ancestral graveyards

each moment stacked
like books of light
or ancestral graveyards
true to spacetime

like books of light
the science of feeling
is true to spacetime
or scattered matter

this science of feeling
the history tapes
or scattered matter
in uncertain glass you

Pastoral

THEME:	nature/bucolic life
FORM:	two octaves
RHYME SCHEME:	optional
METRE:	optional
POEM LENGTH:	16 lines

BACKGROUND:
— pastoral poetry traditionally seeks to celebrate simplicity of country life
— early pastorals often based on fictional place (for example: Arcadia/Eden)
— roots in early Greek literature
    see Theocritus > *Idylls*
— Virgil as major source (Roman) > *Eclogues*
— later embraced philosophical/political concerns re civilisation & natural world
— development of natural world as idealised realm > Romantic era
— contemporary pastorals may embrace grief (for example: deforestation or urbanisation)

FORM:
— 1st octave = description
— 2nd octave = emotional/political/social response

TASK:
— choose a natural area you are familiar with > creek/shoreline/mountain/gully
— note physical/geological/botanical features > be specific
— research history if relevant
— focus on imagery as impelling force for personal response
— construct poem which eulogises or laments chosen landscape

READING:
— Robert Adamson 'Into Forest' *P&W Anthology of Australian Poetry*
— John Anderson '*the forest set out like the night*' *Australian Poetry Since 1788*
— Gary Catalano 'Pastoral' *www.poetrylibrary.edu.au*
— Philip Hodgins 'The Land Itself' *P&W Anthology of Australian Poetry*
— John Kinsella 'Map: Land Subjected to Inundation' *Macquarie PEN Anthology*
— Anthony Lawrence 'Wildflowers, Tallering Station' *New and Selected Poems*
— Vicki Viidikas 'The country as an answer' *P&W Anthology of Australian Poetry*
— Judith Wright 'South of My Days' *Macquarie PEN Anthology*

South of My Days
—Judith Wright

South of my days' circle, part of my blood's country,
rises that tableland, high delicate outline
of bony slopes wincing under the winter,
low trees, blue-leaved and olive, outcropping granite—
clean, lean, hungry country. The creek's leaf-silenced,
willow choked, the slope a tangle of medlar and crabapple
branching over and under, blotched with a green lichen;
and the old cottage lurches in for shelter.

O cold the black-frost night. The walls draw in to the warmth
and the old roof cracks its joints; the slung kettle
hisses a leak on the fire. Hardly to be believed that summer
will turn up again some day in a wave of rambler roses,
thrust its hot face in here to tell another yarn—
a story old Dan can spin into a blanket against the winter.
Seventy years of stories he clutches round his bones.
Seventy years are hived in him like old honey.

Droving that year, Charleville to the Hunter,
nineteen-one it was, and the drought beginning;
sixty head left at the McIntyre, the mud round them
hardened like iron; and the yellow boy died
in the sulky ahead with the gear, but the horse went on,
stopped at the Sandy Camp and waited in the evening.
It was the flies we seen first, swarming like bees.
Came to the Hunter, three hundred head of a thousand—
cruel to keep them alive—and the river was dust.

Or mustering up in the Bogongs in the autumn
when the blizzards came early. Brought them down; we brought them
down, what aren't there yet. Or driving for Cobb's on the run
up from Tamworth—Thunderbolt at the top of Hungry Hill,
and I give him a wink. I wouldn't wait long, Fred,
not if I was you; the troopers are just behind,
coming for that job at the Hillgrove. He went like a luny,
him on his big black horse.
                    Oh, they slide and they vanish
as he shuffles the years like a pack of conjuror's cards.
True or not, it's all the same; and the frost on the roof
cracks like a whip, and the back-log breaks into ash.
Wake, old man. This is winter, and the yarns are over.
No-one is listening.
                    South of my days' circle
I know it dark against the stars, the high lean country
full of old stories that still go walking in my sleep.

Prose Poem

THEME:	a virtue/a sin
FORM:	paragraph block
RHYME SCHEME:	none
METRE:	none
POEM LENGTH:	maximum 20 lines

FORM:
— prose poetry (generally) comprises complete sentences
— lines turn naturally as they reach right-hand margin > thus, the artifice of the line
   turn in conventional poetry is not relevant here
— paragraph block may be right-hand justified
— characteristics of a prose poem *should* include:
   unity within brevity
   poetic quality despite lack of line breaks
   sustained intensity
   contracted emotion
   compactness
— characteristics of a prose poem *may* include:
   a sense of patterning
   rhythmic/figural repetition
   metaphor
   internal spatial interest
   wit

TASK:
— select one of the seven heavenly virtues
   (chastity, temperance, charity, diligence, patience, kindness, humility)
   or one of the seven deadly sins
   (wrath, greed, sloth, pride, lust, envy, gluttony)
— research virtue/sin in terms of grace/damnation > implications for life
— construct a context in which to explore virtue/sin
   fairytale
   personal story
   eyewitness account
   prayer
   confession
   news report
   parable
   fable
— do not be misled by the oxymoronic name > this is a poem!

READING:
— Gary Catalano 'A River and Some Hills' *Australian Poetry Since 1788*
— Rebecca Edwards 'Dark Poems' *New Music*
— Misbah Khokhar 'Ruins' *Contemporary Asian Australian Poets*
— Geoff Page 'Seven Sins' *www.poetrylibrary.edu.au*
— John A. Scott 'Polka' *P&W Anthology of Australian Poetry*
— Charles Simic *The World Doesn't End*
— Alex Skovron *Autographs*

Dark Poems
—Rebecca Edwards

I don't want to pull these black worms out of me. It hurts. The white page nags
like a headache for parrotfeathers and flowers. The flowers outside the window
in the room where I make tea, cluster red-taloned, fierce in their green nests.
Somedays the red teapot is what I cling to, like a mother. Its warmth,
its comforting abundance, against the dark.
'Write something happy. Don't you ever write happy?' the students of literature
ask me. They don't want to read about worms. They want kisses, and no teeth
in them. Just the tip of the tongue, not its bloody, veined root.
You kiss me, and I remember I was so afraid I'd lose you. Now I have, I wonder
did I look too much behind, or too far ahead?
These boys, they don't want seers. They want coca-cola. In the dark.

Ruins
—Misbah Khokhar

Sparrows find shade in throne rooms, and along balconies at night the
goats find beds of soft hay in doorless temples. In tiled bathhouses, in
subterranean granaries, in domed towers with steep steps, in cavernous
antechambers, a hundred families thrive between walls of flayed silk
livid with dye. When their cooking fires are lit, the walls glow like the
inside of a blood orange and the pockmarked ruins are best seen from
afar. The farmers and goat herders, spice-makers, dyers of wool, asleep
in golden bedchambers, asleep for a thousand years, rise to survey their
kingdom. Children abandon their families and gather in chambers to plot
their transgressions with blackened sticks on rotting walls. They burn the
bones of dead birds, pulling at each others' limbs with savage laughter,
and for a thousand years they all sleep and wake to find each door open
and every golden tower is theirs.

Refrain Poem

THEME:	missive to child-self
FORM:	3 quintains (with refrain)
RHYME SCHEME:	aabba
METRE:	none
TENSE:	present
STANCE:	2nd person ("you")

FORM:
— a refrain is a line (or lines) repeated verbatim
   (referred to as 'incremental repetition' if *not* verbatim)
— also known as 'burden', 'chorus', 'repetend'
— usually occurs at regular intervals
— typically found at end of stanza or verse

TASK:
— compose a poem in three 5-line stanzas
— repeat 1st line of poem as each stanza's final line >
   A, 2, 3, 4, A / 6, 7, 8, 9, A / 11, 12, 13, 14, A (see Longfellow's poem)
— address poem to yourself as child (any age)
— speak from present day adult perspective
— focus on a specific emotional crisis/hurdle
— attempt to encourage child-self to persevere >
   "everything is alright in the end . . ."
   "all things pass . . ."
   "I am okay now . . ."
— adopt a tone both philosophical & loving > emotional precision

READING:
— Merlinda Bobis 'Litany' *Contemporary Asian Australian Poets*
— Grant Caldwell 'across the sea' *glass clouds*
— Anita Heiss 'I'm Not Racist But . . .' *Penguin Anthology of Australian Poetry*
— Louisa Lawson 'God Give Me Gold' *P&W Anthology of Australian Poetry*
— Henry Wadsworth Longfellow 'The Tide Rises, the Tide Falls'
   www.poetryfoundation.org
— Geoff Page 'Grit' *Australian Poetry Since 1788*
— Dorothy Porter 'Bluebottles' *Penguin Anthology of Australian Poetry*
— Kenneth Slessor 'Five Bells' *P&W Anthology of Australian Poetry*
— Dylan Thomas 'And Death Shall Have No Dominion' *www.poemhunter.com*
— Francis Webb 'A Man' *P&W Anthology of Australian Poetry*

The Tide Rises, the Tide Falls
—Henry Wadsworth Longfellow

The tide rises, the tide falls,
The twilight darkens, the curlew calls;
Along the sea-sands damp and brown
The traveller hastens toward the town,
    And the tide rises, the tide falls.

Darkness settles on roofs and walls,
But the sea, the sea in the darkness calls;
The little waves, with their soft, white hands,
Efface the footprints in the sands,
    And the tide rises, the tide falls.

The morning breaks; the steeds in their stalls
Stamp and neigh, as the hostler calls;
The day returns, but nevermore
Returns the traveller to the shore,
    And the tide rises, the tide falls.

God Give Me Gold
—Louisa Lawson

God give me gold that I may test
The blessed sweets of perfect rest,
For I am ill and hotly pressed.
    God give me gold!

God give me gold that I may ease
The sorrow that the city sees—
I cannot help the least of these.
    God give me gold!

God give me gold that I may buy
The thing for which my soul doth sigh—
For human love, else, Lord, I die.
    God give me gold!

Senryu

THEME:	a human foible
FORM:	17 syllables *or less*
POEM LENGTH:	3 lines (5/7/5)
METRE:	none
RHYME SCHEME:	none
TENSE:	usually present
TITLE:	none

—   see HAIKU

BACKGROUND:
—   named after C18th inventor (Senryu Karai)

FORM:
—   shares same formal structure as haiku (without *kigo* or *kireji*)
—   subject is *human* nature, particularly dark side
—   style is 'flash fiction' (snapshot of situation, layered with meaning)
—   tone is cynical/black humour

—   example by Alex Skovron:

Ieku

Slipping into sleep:
what a mysterious process.
One moment you're. . .

(NB. *hai* translates into English as "yes", *ie* as "no"!)

TASK:
—   choose a human weakness/shortcoming/flaw
—   compose a number of senryu
—   concentrate on compressing a story . . .

READING:
—   Bruce Beaver 'Kafka Senryu' *The Long Game*
—   Grant Caldwell 'haiku & senryu' (excerpts) *glass clouds*
—   Rick Gabb (unpublished)
—   Matt Hetherington *sweeping the dust*
—   Senryu Karai
—   Les Murray 'Senryu' *Collected Poems*
—   Harold Stewart 'Senryu—Laughing River-willows' *Australian Poetry Since 1788*

untitled
—Senryu Karai

Catching him—
you see the robber
is your son

Senryu
—Les Murray

Just two hours after
Eternal Life pills came out
someone took thirty.

from haiku & senryu
—Grant Caldwell

diary entry—
december 7th
buy new diary

kissing her—
my hat
blows off

untitled
—Rick Gabb

I took my dog
to the Dalmatian Show:
Spot where are you?

Sequence Poem

THEME: open
FORM: open/free
SECTIONS: minimum 3
POEM LENGTH: maximum 3 pages
RHYME SCHEME: optional
METRE: optional
STANCE: vary section to section
TENSE: vary section to section

FORM:
— a sequence poem is a sustained poetic work in sections
— sections allow for variation in angle/idea/tense/timeframe/narrative stance
— sections may be demarcated by:
   numerals (Roman or Arabic)
   asterisks, or other dinkus
   subtitles
   years/dates/times
   other

TASK:
— consider ways in which to maintain burden of subject over sustained length
— investigate appropriate ways to break up poem
— sections to be treated as semi-independent

READING:
— Bruce Beaver 'To the Divine Mystery'
   (sections separated by Roman numerals) *The Long Game*
— Samuel Taylor Coleridge 'The Rime of the Ancient Mariner'
   (sections separated by headings "Part 1", "Part 2", etc.) *Norton Anthology of Poetry*
— Anthony Lawrence 'Signatures'
   (sections separated by dinkus) *Signal Flare*
— Francis Ponge 'Water'
   (prose poems separated by asterisks) *100 Great Poems of the Twentieth Century*
— Ron Pretty 'Kelly Street Weekly'
   (sonnets separated by days of the week) *what the afternoon knows*
— Walt Whitman 'When Lilacs Last in the Dooryard Bloom'd'
   (sections separated by Arabic numerals) *Norton Anthology of Poetry*

from Kelly Street Weekly
—Ron Pretty

Monday

This cottage has taken root above the steps
with windows open to the night sky.

It is ringed by the buildings of the city,
like the battlements of some huge castle.

The bulk of the mountain is unseen behind
the scatter of lights that climb towards it.

This evening the wind is rattling the glass,
clouds travel so fast the rain is horizontal.

Handel is at his music to the night sky
polishing the fleeting stars, fluting with the wind.

The strings dance with the waving trees; the oboe
and every light on the hillside seems to sing.

The city at night is spellbound, a creature
of lights and music and scarifying wind.

Tuesday

Too much light. Neon floods the space, windows
reflect the room & not the world outside where
the wind sings & rain rattles the roof of this
small cottage that sits above the steps.
At night & in the morning I hear footsteps passing,
voices of children calling, a woofer like
a bullfrog. But tonight it's just the weather
calling me as I sit here in this bright room
wishing for candles, the quivering whisper of light
I hear my mysteries in, the muses at their play.
When the world has stopped its stalking
down the colonnades of memory, I'll light
a small wax candle to the future; I'll see
in that dim flame the shapes I trace & try to name.

Wednesday

The old house creaks in the wind like
a barquentine. Shiver me doorframes!
The wind at night blows sleet off the mountain
—or so it seems. I put on jumpers, extra socks

and find myself rejoicing in the blast. I think
I'm tired of endless summer, the warmth
that shows us what we're headed for. I want
the icy wind that brings tears to my eyes

joy to my frost-bitten heart. The plane trees bend,
their lights fling like demented flamencos
on the quays and I rejoice to watch them
and the sleet that beats upon my panes.

The house on Kelly Street hunkers against the blast
and I have found in icy rain my place at last.

Thursday

Down past Battery Point I walked, and round
to Sandy Bay. The Casino stuck its thumb up
at me, where once I'd had a Christmas dinner.
The yachts rocked in the glittering windswept bay.

That wind blew paper at me as I crossed
the street and made for the mayhem at Woolies.
Checked out with my shoddy goods, poorer
though not wiser, I was surprised to see

that wind had fetched the rain. *That's Hobart*
the locals said as they raised umbrellas and ran
with the breeze. I pushed uphill, rain in my face,
my smallgoods floating in my good green bag

until I reached the top of Kelly Street. And then
as I passed the roses, the damn sun shone again.

from Signatures
—Anthony Lawrence

Devotional literature, translated from the inter-tidal zone
and signed in the red
throat bellows of a frigate bird, like a black paper lantern
a late sun sets fire to.

~

A death sentence, commuted
to twelve hours of agony
after being underwritten
in a fine-grained film of tropical sand

138

stamped by a low-tide wader
who'd ignored the sign suggesting footwear
and whose voice was reduced
to diminishing yelps
when the dorsal nibs of a stone fish
made light work of a calloused heel.

~

The disinfected loom
of a cardio-thoracic surgeon
who leans in
to sign off on a complex procedure
with green thread
stitching the wall of an artery
hung with bad forgeries of Miro.

~

The flash and gleam of isobars
on the face of a rainsquall
completed by the signature flourish
of a raptor lifting away
from a roadside window display of sweetmeats.

~

Your enduring signature, your smile
still visible in the depth of field
absence makes from old emulsion
when the shutter and mirror caught and held you there.

~

The worn cursive script of a bivalve's passage
from sandstone ledger to algal receipt
ending at the sharps deposit box
of a rock pool filled with urchins.

Sestina

THEME:	rite of passage
FORM:	6 sestets & 3-line envoi with lexical repetition
POEM LENGTH:	39 lines
METRE:	none
RHYME SCHEME:	none

BACKGROUND:
— C12th French troubadour form (Arnaut Daniel)
— aim to outdo one another with technical dexterity at court
— arrived in English late C16th > popularised C19th

FORM:
— complex fixed verse form
— originally syllabic, often in iambic pentameter
— 6 teleutons (end-words) utilised in elaborate set pattern
— 6-line stanzas = 123456 / 615243 / 364125 / 532614 / 451362 / 246531
— envoi = 531 *or* 135, with medial 246

TASK:
— begin with five loosely related teleutons & one 'rogue', for example:
  1 "sea" (see/seas)
  2 "moon" (noun/verb)
  3 "light" (lit/lightly/lighter/alight/lights/noun/verb)
  4 "dream" (dreamer/dreamed/dreams)
  5 "fish" (fishes/fishing/verb/noun/singular/plural)
  6 "wherever"
— endeavour to convey sense of moving forward albeit circuitously
— envoi to be treated as something like coda/epilogue
— *occasional* variant spellings/tenses/contractions/extensions permitted, in order to facilitate flow & conceal form
— teleutons may be used alternatively as noun/verb or singular/plural (see above)
— enjambment encouraged
— subject suggestions:
  first kiss/dance/cigarette/fight
  getting driver's license
  killing an animal
  menstruation/menopause/losing virginity
  leaving/moving home
  losing a parent/child
  immigration

READING:
— Elizabeth Bishop 'Sestina' *The Complete Poems*
— Stephen Fry 'Arnaut's Algorithm' *The Ode Less Travelled*
— Alan Gould 'The Vinlanders—Six Character Studies' *The Past Completes Me*
— L.K. Holt 'Half Sestina' *Man Wolf Man*
— Anthony Lawrence 'The Drive' *P&W Anthology of Australian Poetry*
— Tom Shapcott 'Australian Horizons' *P&W Anthology of Australian Poetry*
— Alex Skovron 'How (Not) to Write a Sestina' *Divan #5*

How (Not) to Write a Sestina
—Alex Skovron

Of all the structures we labour to conceal
(yes, that should suffice for an opening line)
the one perhaps most treacherous to handle
is that old thirty-niner, the sestina:
it has been the undoing of many a fine poet
otherwise superb at avoiding the obvious.

Well, let's examine this notion, 'the obvious'
(that was a case of exposing to conceal).
First of all, the more finicky the poet,
the greater the agony to make certain each line
of each stanza of that putative sestina,
and every closure, will open like a handle

into the next—so yes, we turn the handle
(since to turn it seems fitting and obvious)
and enter, innocent, those Pillars of Sestina
all the marbled ikons are looming to conceal,
as we proceed open-mouthed down the line
of columns and catafalques like a drugged poet;

a poet replete with reverence, transfigured poet
(whose suggestibility is thus safer to handle),
all our linear perspectives falling into line.
Second, and a point that ought to be obvious,
those six leit-echoes, in order to conceal
themselves, must not make us yell out 'Sestina!'

as soon as the first one happens, 'Look, sestina!'
(that was both irony and cheek: I'm a cheeky poet);
so the words should be somewhat escapable, to conceal
their persistence: contrast *hippo* with *handle*!
Third, canny distractions both arcane and obvious,
like felonious homophones that don't quite align,

can be used, or the parenthetic slotting of a line
(like the ones I've smuggled into this sestina)
which recurs for some reason other than obvious.
Above all, it's suicide for the unsuspecting poet
to lock himself into a maze he can neither handle
—or herself/she—nor shed, squirming to conceal

line after line (desperate to finish), a sinking poet
in a quicksand of sestina, at a loss how to handle
the envoi, the ending, the agony too obvious to conceal.

Signature Poem

THEME:	open
FORM:	open
RHYME SCHEME:	optional
METRE:	optional
STANCE:	personal choice
TENSE:	personal choice
POEM LENGTH:	maximum one page

TASK:
— write a poem using content/form of choice
— exercise & exploit freedom in all aspects of composition
— employ devices/imagery/sentiments elemental to your specific 'voice'
— approach poem as representative of your poetry in general: *the* poem you might be 'remembered by', that somehow sums up your oeuvre
— choosing one's 'signature poem' is usually beyond one's control
— pretend you are 'the world' > that you have control to choose what posterity would otherwise dictate
— dig deep for what you want to say > *how* you want to say it
— consider layout/vocabulary/pace/tone
— build your perfect poem: this is your chance to sing!
— WARNING: take care not to 'cliché' yourself . . .
— be prepared to discuss your poem in the context of your poetry as a whole

READING:
— your own poems!

Warm-Up Exercises

—LINE TURN EXERCISE*

Reformat the following two 'sentences' into poems > consider visuals, rhythm, possible rhymes . . .

1.
As the cat climbed over the top of the jamcloset first the right forefoot carefully then the hind stepped down into the pit of the empty flowerpot

2.
of all things under our blonder than blondest star the most mysterious (eliena, my dear) is this—how anyone so gay possibly could die

—EYE RHYME EXERCISE*

There are eight pronunciations of the syllable "ough". Write a one-sentence poem containing words with as many different "ough" sounds as possible.

—MICRO-SONNET EXERCISE

Using only fourteen words, write a micro-sonnet with "a window" as your theme.

—OULIPIAN EXERCISE

Write a short poem describing a pivotal moment in history. Rewrite, avoiding the letter "e", while maintaining sense, style, pace and tone.

—MONOSYLLABIC EXERCISE

Write a poem about sleep, employing words of only one syllable.

—TRANSLATION EXERCISE

Rewrite a short unrhymed poem by a well-known poet. Replace structure, images and metaphors, while staying true to original poet's intentions.

—LEFT BRAIN EXERCISE

Write a poem about your country of birth, using your non-dominant hand.

*see back of book...

Simile Poem

THEME:	a fruit
FORM:	octaves (each consisting of 2 linked chiasmic quatrains)
RHYME SCHEME:	abbacddc
METRE:	none
POEM LENGTH:	2 stanzas
TENSE:	present

FORM:
— 8-line stanzas
— 'simile' > figure of speech in which two fundamentally unlike things are explicitly compared, usually in a phrase beginning with "like" or "as"
— the following are common similes (clichés):
  [the fairground was] as silent as the grave
  [I've been] working like a dog
  [his sense of humour is] as dry as a bone
  [your excuse is] like the sound of one hand clapping
  [their teacher is] as hard as nails
  [the new puppy is] as good as gold
  [her character is] as straight as an arrow
  [the brothers are] like two peas in a pod
  [my love is] like a red, red rose
  [he eats] like a pig

TASK:
— exercise in sensual description
— select a fruit
— examine/document fruit in terms of sight/sound/taste/scent/touch
— be as specific as possible
— employ similes as required
— take care not to confuse with 'metaphor' (see METAPHOR POEM)
— avoid common similes > write your own!
— research fruit > characteristics/history/symbolism/anecdotes/legend/myth
— construct personal story around fruit
— collate description/research/story into one fluid poem
— arouse each of the (reader's) senses while unfolding narrative
— assume reader has never tasted/seen fruit before
— attempt to 'replace' fruit with poem . . .

READING:
— Alison Croggon 'The Elwood Organic Fruit and Vegetable Shop' *P&W Anthology of Australian Poetry*
— Sarah Day 'Apples' *Grass Notes*
— Robert Gray 'A Bowl of Pears' *Coast Road*
— Peter Kirkpatrick 'The Mango Suckers' *New Music*
— Stanley Kunitz 'My Mother's Pears' *Poets Laureate Anthology*
— Yann Martel *Beatrice and Virgil* pp. 44-51 (novel)
— Vicki Raymond 'King Pineapple' *Australian Poetry Since 1788*
— Christina Rossetti *Goblin Market*
— Peter Steele 'Pomegranate' *Australian Poetry Since 1788*

A Bowl of Pears
—Robert Gray

Swarthy as oilcloth and as paunched
as Sancho Panza
wearing a beret's little stalk
the pear

itself suggests the application of some rigor
the finest blade
from the knife drawer
here

to freshen it is one slice and then another
the north fall south fall
facets of glacier
the snow-clean juice with a slight crunch that is sweet

I find lintels and plinths of white marble
clean angled
where there slides
the perfume globule

a freshness
like the breeze that is felt upon
the opening
of day's fan

Enku
sculptor of pine stumps
revealed the ten thousand Buddhas with his attacks
the calligraphic axe

Rationalised shape shaped with vertical strokes
I have made of your jowled
buttocks
a squareness neatly pelvic

A Sunday of rain
and like a drain
a pipe that was agog and is now chock-a-block the limber thunder
rebounds and bounds

it comes pouring down
a funnel the wrong way around
broadcasts
its buffoon militance over the houses all afternoon

Undone
the laces of rain
dangle on the windows
now slicing iron

a butcher is sharpening
the light
of his favourite knife
its shimmers carving stripes into the garden

And I have carved the pear-shaped head
with eyes
close set
as pips that Picasso saw his poor

friend who had gone
to war
a cubist
snowman the fragrant and fatal Apollinaire

Pomegranate
—Peter Steele

for Adrienne Clarke

Given the puckered crown and the sleek orb,
        a warlord's reach makes all the sense
those courtiers of doom can manage. "Sour,
        yet sweet" was Bolingbroke's device,
the yellow nob brought home from Moorish kings,
        England astringent in his grasp.

Still, while our feckless breed pays out its danegeld
        year by year to the Prince of Darkness—
so many bodies drained of their dearest blood—
        a fresher image buds to rebuke
that yield of heartlessness, the bright grenade:
        to the cupped palm of Sandro's Madonna

the child's astonished hand goes out, and fingers
        a little globe of lavishness.
The company about have not so much
        as a smile between them: yet all sweetens,
gravity blossoming into joy, the mind
        cheered as by juice blended with snow.

The Elwood Organic Fruit and Vegetable Shop
—Alison Croggon

I will go walking in Elwood with my mind as smooth as a marrow
winking at the unruffled sky throwing its light down for free
letting the gardens exude their well-groomed scents and thinking
       everything good
to the Elwood Organic Fruit and Vegetable Shop:
for the counter is democratically in the centre and everyone smiles
for people go on with the civil business of buying and selling under the
       handwritten notices
for bawling children are solaced with grapes and handled to leave no bruises
for the mangoes are soft yellow thighs and the strawberries are klaxons of
       sweetness
for the mignonette purses its frilly lips and snowpeas pout their
       discreet bellies and the melons hug their quirky shapes under their
       marvellous rinds
for onions ringing their coppery globes and o the silver shallots
       and the hairy trumpets of leeks
for the cabbages folding crisp linens and the broccolis
       blooming in purple tulles and the dense green skirts of lettuces
for peaches like breasts of angels and passionfruits hard and
       dark and bursting with seed in your palm
for the dull gold flesh of pontiacs and knotty umbers of yams
       and new potatoes like the heels of babies
for the tubs of sweet william and heart-lifting freesias and orchids
       damp and beautiful as clitoral kisses
for poignant basil and maiden-haired fennel and prim blue-lipped
       rosemary and o! irrepressible mint!
how they nestle up the vegetables, promising them the fragrance of
       their ardour!
the marriages which await them! the lips that moisten to meet
       them! glorious speech of the earth!

Snapshot Poem

THEME: photographic sequence
FORM: free (3–4 sections)
RYHME SCHEME: none
METRE: none
POEM LENGTH: maximum 23 lines

—   see SEQUENCE POEM

TASK:
—   construct poem based on three or four photographs
—   photographs should be related in some way:
       annual event
       seasons
       childhood
       homes
       holidays
       pets
—   avoid simply explaining pictures
—   aim beyond surface: attempt to reveal what is hidden beneath
—   free form to encourage uninhibited interface between image/memory & language
—   allow one subtitled section per photograph
—   each section variable length (bear in mind 23-line maximum)
—   formatting example:

         TITLE

         i.   *subtitle*

       first section (variable length)
       poem poem poem poem

         ii.   *subtitle*

       second section (variable length)
       poem poem poem poem
       poem poem poem poem

READING:
—   Alan Gould 'Marine Photographs' *The Past Completes Me*
—   Coral Hull 'Landscape Photography with Dogs' *New Music*
—   Judy Johnson 'Photograph of my Great Grandparents, 1880' *Nomadic*
—   Ian McBryde 'The Still Company' *Flank*
—   Peter Porter 'Family Album' *Family Ties*
—   Adrienne Rich 'Snapshots of a Daughter-in-Law' *Norton Anthology of Poetry*
—   Jennifer Strauss 'A Black and White Photo' *Turnrow Anthology*

Family Album
—Peter Porter

Tenable in dreams, here they are twice
as plausible, holding court to the lens,
with nothing to say but the truth.
                    Myself, my mother,
culled from the caucus of summer
by a relative's whim: how did the fat woman
keep so many bees off her howling son?
                    That man, chained to
his gross watch, wearing his waistcoat
like Prometheus his rock, did he edge
to the aerodrome to show he was too
frightened to enter the twentieth century?
                    It makes a good fiction
to leer at their confidence. Something else
would fit in. The light, acid but milky,
along the near shore and the ironclad ferry
touching the stage; Cousin Timperley
walking an ice-cream up to the pines,
Beethoven for supper, everyone upright.
                    Later, dispersal may offer
your motorcade stopping en route to Tibe-
rias,
'This is Cana, so don't check the water
in your radiator'. Over us looms Mount
Gilboa where Saul fell on his sword,
a mortar lob from the red hibiscus
kibbutz, its blond children playing
through the collective afternoon.
                    Pictures from a lost
exhibition. Not the pianola and
the telescope, but a high-backed
Russian chair and the brilliantined
bridegroom asleep after venery.
Or this tribute: 'How we brought
the Good News', key of F Minor,
the house in the corn.
                    That hand, that brown face,
now papery, channelled with heart
disease, the transit of Venus.
Mother and father met here in me
ascribing a terror of photographs
to the lingering snake in the garden.
                    Made objective now
on the lake where the red-eyed fish
walk on wallpaper. O sails of death
that we watched on the river, weeks of rain
when we came to our father's house,
the pictures are ready, shall we walk in?

The Still Company
—Ian McBryde

"With photography, you zero in."
Robert Mapplethorpe

1. *Click*

I want their expressions
to be filled with
more than history.

I want the flattened grass
springing quickly back up

from where their feet fall
as they walk towards me
in black and white.

2. *Click*

It is me. It is
not me. The same vague

determination. Something
different about the eyes,
a sense of having stepped

back without moving.
It is me. It is not me.

3. *Click*

I remember taking
this one of you,
how your eyes slid past

and your small fingers
tightened on the sill.

One odd distant cloud
reflected in the window.
The end of autumn

and a long dust brushed
off suitcases. How I

turned quietly away.
How much more my smiles
have cost since then.

from Marine Photographs
—Alan Gould

Any Two Pictures
(*Schomberg*, 1855)

Begin with this. The painted clipper swings
around its cable in the busy port,
beside a hatch, this free man lost in thought
as morning sunshine gifts the spars like wings.

Move on to this—a sky of mazarine,
the rocks shrug off the ocean like a shawl.
If vessel, crew, distinguished captain all
foundered here once, they did not change the scene.

Between these pictures falls the known event
and falls the shock of its exactitude.
For, being all his self could not prevent,
the self and rocks and vessel all construed
the one necessity, a free man's past,
and *if* and *then* made crystalline at last.

The Wave
(*Blackadder*, 1873)

You disentwined that moment from your lifetime—

needle falling through the nervous hours
through the dogwatch seas that turn obsidian,
wind collecting strength on astral distance,
rogue-wave growing on the windward quarter,
wave that gathers up the world's horizons,
making, like a mother, you its centre . . .

There! Unborn, you see you've always travelled
with one who's shyer, truer, than your selfhood.
Your luck? Your fate? The thing eludes its name
but quietly stands between your life and death.
The wave explodes and drains its everything,
whose cyclone was exact, brought trouble and
a reappearing coast, a town, a berth.

Still Lives
(*Ariel; Thermopylae*, 1872)

I say *No life is still*, and I must face
an equatorial night, the sea black-glass,
the bearded man, not of my era, smoking
at the main rail, a headsail slatting, plucking,
while overhead, remote, exacting stars
pause in their nightly circle. *Only trust us*,
they state, *we are the map that's true, trust us*.
This ship's about to vanish without trace.

I say *No life is still*, but tilt the world
to Sunda Strait; a ship of green and gold
ghosts in the ticklish airs, the darks of sail
are limp, the sea babbles softly to the keel,
a scent of cheroot lingers in the air.
So calm, so still, how can the quick elsewhere
of weathers be imagined, the eye disengage
from the plucking noises, these fixtures of an age?

I want the fullest picture, perhaps because
it is, like God's, a knowledge that's no use.
But tilting dawnward are the straining topsails,
the flag of smoke that pricks the horizontals.
No lives are still, yet lives live there *and* here.
A ship glides home, the thronging docksides cheer,
while on a mainrail veers the programmed wave.
I see the drowning men I cannot save.

35° S 5° W
(*Sobraon*, 1883)

The woman travelling alone will leap
with all her skirts and reasons to the sea.
This is a Sunday night. She'll not be found.

Focus on that instant. Discourse issues
from the lit saloon, while under her
the wake is bulbing madly like blown skirts.
Behind her rope and sail obey their theory.

Yes, all geometry upholds her here.
Also, imply no failures, only that
her years are fixed upon this chemistry
as marks upon a map. For the past

is so exact. It's *this* that moves her most.
Sad beyond all gesture now she falls
from what made her into what now makes her.

Sonnet (Petrarchan)

THEME:	argument/crisis
FORM:	quatorzain (chiasmic octave & sestet)
POEM LENGTH:	14 lines
METRE:	generally iambic pentameter
RHYME SCHEME:	abbaabba/cdecde
TONE:	dignified (exposition & response)

— see METRICAL POEM

BACKGROUND:
— 'sonnet' from Italian *sonetto* (little song or sound)
— Sicilian sonnet dates back to C12th
— rigorously developed by Francesco Petrarch in Tuscany (C14th)
— Petrarchan sonnet also known as Italian sonnet

FORM:
— octave (8 lines) & sestet (6 lines):
    octave = strong opening question or statement
    stanza break (volta, meaning "turn")
    sestet = emotional/intellectual resolution
— sestet rhymes cdecde, cdcdcd, or any combination which avoids final couplet
— 5 rhymes

TASK:
— construct a Petrarchan sonnet > 'argument'
— focus on volta as turning point in poem

READING:
— Kevin Brophy 'Walking towards sunset' *P&W Anthology of Australian Poetry*
— Zora Cross 'Love Sonnet XLIX' *P&W Anthology of Australian Poetry*
— Stephen Edgar 'A Divine Comedy' *lost in the foreground*
— Gwen Harwood 'In the Park' *P&W Anthology of Australian Poetry*
— Francesco Petrarch 'The Canzoniere' (sonnets 1–10) *The Poetry of Petrarch*
— Gig Ryan 'When I consider' *Australian Poetry Since 1788*
— William Wordsworth 'Composed upon Westminster Bridge, September 3, 1802' *Seven Centuries*

Composed upon Westminster Bridge, September 3, 1802
—William Wordsworth

Earth has not anything to show more fair:
Dull would he be of soul who could pass by
A sight so touching in its majesty:
This City now doth, like a garment, wear
The beauty of the morning; silent, bare,
Ships, towers, domes, theatres, and temples lie
Open unto the fields, and to the sky;
All bright and glittering in the smokeless air.
Never did sun more beautifully steep
In his first splendour, valley, rock, or hill;
Ne'er saw I, never felt, a calm so deep!
The river glideth at his own sweet will:
Dear God! the very houses seem asleep;
And all that mighty heart is lying still!

Love Sonnet XLIX
—Zora Cross

In me there is a vast and lonely place
Where none, not even you, have walked in sight.
A wide, still vale of solitude and light,
Where Silence echoes into ebbing space.
And there I creep at times and hide my face,
While in myself I fathom wrong and right,
And all the timeless ages of the night
That sacred silence of my soul I pace.
And when from there I come to you, love-swift,
My mouth hot-edged with kisses fresh as wine
Often I find your longings all asleep
And unresponsive from my grasp you drift.
Ah, Love, you, too, seek solitude like mine,
And soul from soul the secret seems to keep.

Sonnet (Shakespearean)

THEME:	love
FORM:	quatorzain (3 quatrains & final couplet)
POEM LENGTH:	14 lines
METRE:	generally iambic pentameter
RHYME SCHEME:	abab/cdcd/efef/gg
TONE:	imagistic/lyrical

—   see METRICAL POEM, SONNET (Petrarchan)

BACKGROUND:
— sonnet arrived in England early C16th (Thomas Wyatt)
— final rhyming couplet introduced
— further developed late C16th (Shakespeare)
— Shakespearean sonnet also known as Elizabethan or English sonnet

FORM:
— 4 units > 3 quatrains + couplet (Q_1, Q_2, Q_3, C)
— a 'key word' may be repeated within each unit as a connective device
— couplet = declamatory > defining moment of sonnet
— couplet must 'tie' with preceding poem, for example: repetition of key (or other) word/s; semantic continuity/discord; temporal thread/contrast
— couplet should be treated as coda (the preceding 3 quatrains a complete poem in themselves)
— 7 rhymes > NO rhyme repetition
— NB. a volta between the second & third quatrains is still present, despite new structure (see Shakespeare's sonnets)

TASK:
— construct a Shakespearean sonnet > 'love'
— be athletic as possible with rhyme variations
— include wit (for example: puns, riddles, anagrams)
— attempt iambic pentameter
— tie ends together neatly in final couplet
— why not attempt a first draft in an hour! (see Keats' 'On the Grasshopper and Cricket', written in quick contest with friend, Leigh Hunt)

READING:
— Vincent Buckley 'Stroke' (section 6 > 18-line sonnet) *P&W Anthology of Australian Poetry*
— Alan Gould 'An Interrogator's Opening Remarks' *P&W Anthology of Australian Poetry*
— Philip Hodgins 'The Birds' *Australian Poetry Since 1788*
— Martin Johnston 'Vernal Equinox' *Australian Poetry Since 1788*
— Vicki Raymond 'On Seeing the First Flasher' *Australian Poetry Since 1788*
— William Shakespeare 'Sonnet 18' ("Shall I compare thee . . .") *Seven Centuries*
— Ian Templeman 'My Father's Letter' *Family Ties*

Sonnet 18
—William Shakespeare

Shall I compare thee to a Summers day?
Thou art more lovely and more temperate:
Rough windes do shake the darling buds of Maie,
And Sommers lease hath all too short a date:
Sometime too hot the eye of heaven shines,
And often is his gold complexion dimm'd,
And every faire from faire some-time declines,
By chance, or natures changing course untrim'd:
But thy eternall Sommer shall not fade,
Nor loose possession of that faire thou ow'st,
Nor shall death brag thou wandr'st in his shade,
When in eternall lines to time thou grow'st,
   So long as men can breath or eyes can see,
   So long lives this, and this gives life to thee.

from Stroke
—Vincent Buckley

VI

The roofs are lit with rain.
Winter. In that dark glow,
Now, as three months ago,
I pray that he'll die sane.

On tiles or concrete path
The old wheeling the old,
For whom, in this last world,
Hope is an aftermath,

And the damp trees extend
Branch and thorn. We live
As much as we believe.
All things covet an end.

Once, on the Kerrie road,
I drove with him through fire.
Now, in the burnt cold year,
He drains off piss and blood,

His wounded face tube-fed,
His arm strapped to a bed.

Sonnet (modern)

THEME:	open
FORM:	quatorzain
METRE:	optional
RHYME SCHEME:	optional
TONE:	open

—   see SONNET (Petrarchan), SONNET (Shakespearean)

BACKGROUND:
—   sonneteers consistently tantalised by possibilities of form
—   Meredithian sonnet > George Meredith (16 lines) > anti-love
—   curtal > Gerard Manley Hopkins (10½ lines)
—   micro-sonnet = 14 *words*

FORM:
—   quatorzaine (14-line poem)

TASK:
—   construct a modern sonnet > open theme
—   creatively explore/exploit 14-line format
—   rhyme scheme not necessary . . .

READING:
—   John Ashbery 'Lost Sonnet' *Planisphere*
—   Billy Collins 'Sonnet' *Poets Laureate Anthology*
—   L.K. Holt 'Heads/Tails' *Keeps*
—   Gerard Manley Hopkins 'Pied Beauty' *www.poetryfoundation.org*
—   Mal McKimmie 'doctordeath.com' *Poetileptic*
—   George Meredith 'Modern Love: I' *www.poetryfoundation.org*
—   James Merrill 'The Broken Home' (varied sonnet sequence) *Collected Poems*
—   Geoff Page (ed.) *Indigo Book of Modern Australian Sonnets*
—   George Starbuck 'Sonnet with a Different Letter at the End of Every Line', 'Space-Saver Sonnets' *The Works*
—   John Tranter 'Sonnet 55: A Hard Art' *Australian Poetry Since 1788*

—   view/interact   *http://www.cranberrydesigns.com/poetry/sonnet/examples.htm*

Sonnet 55: A Hard Art
—John Tranter

Waiting and waiting, there's an end to it.
Eating bad food, sleeping on the floor,
there's an end to that too. One day
your enemies reach out of your head quickly
and take you to the cold and dirty places,
and you're too old for that sort of thing.
The bad music keeps you there, and makes you cruel,
and you are the loved one you are least kind to.

Waiting and waiting for the good weather,
there's a hard art in that, and a sour man—
too old for that sort of punishment—does it badly.
But one day you wake up and go back home and if you're
tough and lucky you leave most of it behind.
Eating good food, accepting kindness—there's an art in that.

Heads/Tails
—L.K. Holt

I join the wellspring of heads up the subway stairs
onto the street sharpened in the light's new bent.
A skull is so makeshiftly wrought! The data entering
boorishly raw, to be civilised and polished by
the artful tail-flicks of neurons; tiny Pygmalions.

When a mind takes on all the sense tasks, the body
just goes and abides by a trifle of laws, the proprieties
of gravity etcetera, silently, as swimmers and sleepers
unsure of the need for a standardised up . . . .

What crime of passion is the mere thought of you?
Counterwork to the real/ Or its vital principle.
Lovers can but gamble in phenomenology:
with each call, one side of the glistening coin of pupil
is wrong—the other, if not right, will do.

Suspense Poem

THEME:	open
FORM:	block (alternating indents)
RHYME SCHEME:	none
METRE:	none
LINE LENGTH:	personal choice
POEM LENGTH:	maximum 200 words
TENSE:	present

FORM:
— delaying devices may include:
  long sentences
  accumulative description
  repetition of imagery
  varying angles of penultimate moment
  visual/mental asides
  focus on minutiae
  precision of detail
  gradual gathering of fact
  step-by-step 'instructions'
  constant *implication* re eventual outcome
  interplay of cause & effect
  crescendo > becoming louder (tone)
  accelerando > becoming faster (pace)
  alliteration

TASK:
— choose event—real or imaginary—with distinct outcome
— write a poem which *delays* this outcome until very end
— attempt a 'poetry of witness' regardless of narrative stance
— induce uncomfortable reader position > reader as 'trapped' in moment
— choose title representative of eventual outcome > immediate suspense
— *control* pace & tone
— take your time: avoid getting ahead of yourself!

READING:
— Elizabeth Bishop 'The Fish' *The Complete Poems*
— James Dickey 'Falling' *www.poetryfoundation.org*
— Philip Hammial 'Demolition' *www.poetrylibrary.edu.au*
— Jill Jones 'The pure in heart' *Motherlode*
— Josephine Rowe 'In the Boot of Someone's Car' *Australian Poetry Since 1788*
— Jemal Sharah 'Kristallnacht' *Australian Poetry Since 1788*

The pure in heart
—Jill Jones

They have taken babies
and blamed it on dingoes.
They've planted foul words
on the righteous tongues
of six-year old bigots.

They have joined hands
with the makers
of warheads, purification
and sub-Arctic famines.

They have studied love
and found it wanting.

They have flushed their water
through cataracts of ice.
They praise the numbers
in their heavy books.

Some of them watch you,
monitor your garbage
for glimpses of hell.
Be careful, they think
their destiny is to drink
from your children.

In the Boot of Someone's Car
—Josephine Rowe

There is a woman
locked in the boot
of someone's car.
The darkness is pressing down on her
so hard she can't breathe
and she can't be sure
whether she's choking on fear
or petrol fumes
or the darkness.
The driver takes the corners too fast.
It hurts less if she just goes limp.
She can't remember how she got there
but she will be there forever
her voice hoarse from screaming
because I can't think of a way to get her out.
I know that somewhere
there's a cable release

or a toolbox with a crowbar
or a wrench.
She could jemmy the lock.
All she has to do is feel around in the dark
but her hands are tied behind her back
and I don't know what to do with her
once she's out.
I don't even know who the driver is.
So I leave her there
in the boot of someone's car.
I've run out of endings.
I leave women crying on doorsteps.
I leave lonely men
in empty carriages
on last trains to nowhere.
I leave families sleeping
as their houses burn to the ground.
I leave gamblers,
cocaine addicts, failed musicians,
prostitutes, lawyers, fathers,
at the top of buildings,
under bridges,
on freeways, train tracks, rooftops,
on the cracked linoleum floors of
restrooms in fast food restaurants
somewhere in the outer western suburbs,
or chain smoking at kitchen tables
watching the smoke curl up to
twenty five watt Homebrand lightbulbs
that flickflickflicker
as they wait for unfaithful lovers
to return home from work.
And I leave a man
with smoke in his eyes
both hands on the wheel
driving as far away as he can
on ten bucks of fuel
before he breaks down.
He calls me
to ask where we're going from here.
And I tell him that I don't know
because I've run out of endings.
I tell him that I'm sorry,
but there's a woman
locked in the boot
of his car.

Kristallnacht
—Jemal Sharah

Alone in the bush.
Before, they had been singing,
when the car was given a great push
off the road; rain tinkling.

And then she got a fright—
the only one awake;
the others' eyes stayed shut tight
no matter how she'd shake

and shove their arms.
She didn't think of death—
sleep wasn't any harm—
and there was her father's breath,

though harsh, asthmatic, sore.
Locked in a foggy sleep
it might have been a snore.
Except it seemed so deep.

And she—she was awash
with cubes of window-glass,
with one leg safely squashed
in a metal cast;

with such neatly shattered crystal.
Her father loved to buy
goblets, clear as the distilled
water from an eye.

Its rhinestones chained her wrists.
She waited as time passed:
one car sped by—missed
seeing them, it went so fast.

And no-one came to help
in spite of all her cries;
she was stuck there herself,
and adult blandishments were lies—

that to cry help was the proof
against perverts, loss, distress,
that the boy who had cried wolf
was gobbled through excess.

Vague rain, sickness in tides;
neither offered any answers.
Nor, later, did the pride
of howling ambulances.

Syllabic Poem

THEME:	rural life
FORM:	octosyllabic
RHYME SCHEME:	optional
METRE:	none
POEM LENGTH:	2 septets

BACKGROUND:
— syllabic verse more common in Asian & Romance languages than English (English is a stress-timed rather than syllable-timed language . . .)
— not popular in English until C19th

FORM:
— fixed syllable count per line, for example:
pentasyllabic = 5 syllables
heptasyllabic = 7 syllables
octosyllabic = 8 syllables
decasyllabic = 10 syllables
— diphthongs counted as one *or* two syllables > the syllabic poet's best friend!
— diphthong from Greek *diphthongos* (two sounds) > "while", "year", "field"

TASK:
— focus on one aspect/area of country life (positive or negative)
— write two 7-line stanzas comprising 8 syllables per line
— utilise syllable count as structural device around which to organise thought
— attempt to create & maintain sense of *music*

READING:
— Bruce Dawe 'Drifters' *P&W Anthology of Australian Poetry*
— Dorothy Hewett 'Country Idyll' *Penguin Anthology of Australian Poetry*
— Philip Hodgins 'Shooting the Dogs' *P&W Anthology of Australian Poetry*
— Marianne Moore 'The Fish' (1, 3, 9, 6, 8) *100 Great Poems of the Twentieth Century*
— Mudrooroo 'Blotched Country Boy' *Penguin Anthology of Australian Poetry*
— Sylvia Plath 'Mushrooms' (5s) *Seven Centuries*
— Kenneth Slessor 'Country Towns' *P&W Anthology of Australian Poetry*
— Dylan Thomas 'The Force that through the Green Fuse Drives the Flower' (10, 10, 4, 10, 10) *Seven Centuries*
— John Watson 'River Syllabics' (8, 12) *A First Reader*
— Judith Wright 'For a Pastoral Family' *P&W Anthology of Australian Poetry*

The Fish
—Marianne Moore

wade
through black jade.
   Of the crow-blue mussel-shells, one keeps
   adjusting the ash-heaps;
      opening and shutting itself like

an
injured fan.
   The barnacles which encrust the side
   of the wave, cannot hide
      there for the submerged shafts of the

sun
split like spun
   glass, move themselves with spotlight swiftness
   into the crevices—
      in and out, illuminating

the
turquoise sea
   of bodies. The water drives a wedge
   of iron through the iron edge
      of the cliff; whereupon the stars,

pink
rice-grains, ink-
   bespattered jelly-fish, crabs like green
   lilies, and submarine
      toadstools, slide each on the other.

All
external
   marks of abuse are present on this
   defiant edifice—
      all the physical features of

ac-
cident—lack
   of cornice, dynamite grooves, burns, and
   hatchet strokes, these things stand
      out on it; the chasm-side is

dead.
Repeated
   evidence has proved that it can live
   on what can not revive
      its youth. The sea grows old in it.

River Syllabics
—John Watson

It will accommodate all things
will accede to anything   without reason,
within certain limits, namely
that it doesn't much like spilling   over its banks
on to the cows' and plovers' fields;
but that said, it's remarkably   ready in flood
to carry all manner of things
blithely and slowly out to sea:

                                        branches, remnants
of old technologies like sheets
of corrugated iron, and what   at second glance
seems to be a coat, within which
someone is enjoying the sun   with arms outstretched,
whole wattle trees, occasional drums
of kerosene—all pass by with   the same calm haste.

Winter covers the fields in rime
and has a vested interest—no   pun intended—
in the flood insofar as it
suggests its flight towards summer.   Ghost-gums standing
untroubled in the water show
how temporary all this is.   A lemon-tree
too is marooned. It leans out and
has deposited like an egg   in the water
near the bank a single lemon
over which the grey and amber   water runs on.

The river insists always that
it should not only bear but that   it should be seen
to bear its weight in passage. Yet
much of all that it brings downstream   bright with passing
is insubstantial, and between
those occasional boats and limbs   of trees and plants
there is a constant flow
unseen by those on the moored barge   who point and call,
a steady stream of objects from
the hinterland of memory.

                                        Half-lost in weeds
A concrete pier, part of an old
long vanished bridge, resurrecting   symmetry, turns
our gaze to seek its fellow on
the opposite bank. There amongst   spent rushes, crops
not renewed, lie only scattered
stones like a deconstructed wall.   Meanwhile flowing
on round the island, the river,
no advocate of bridges, clears   away excess
from the flood-plain, preoccupied,
intent just to see everything   out to sea, then
to relinquish it in a long

shoal of undecided water.

                                        At that
ambiguous entrance   there is at a certain
uncertain point a tract   of sea and river where
leaf-tannin clearly quite   immiscible with waves
declares an area   several miles across,
brackish, bracken-coloured,   heavy with leaves, in which
it would be hard to tell   where one or the other
began or ended. Soon   all its purpose which bore
the river and with which   it bore its furniture,
all its former resolve   is dissipated and
is at last quite lost. Here   without regular waves
or benefit of banks,   in this vast swimming-pool
where dazzled and dazzling,   bright see-saws of divers
surface and disappear   and under its cloud-glow
the sun cuts grooves across   its yeast-risen surface
turbulence is the rule   and eventually
an equilibrium   is struck in which neither
slowed river nor held sea   is at ease or even
willing to compromise. The river which had once
accommodated such   variety is now
itself uneasily   absorbed. But far upstream
fresh logs are being launched   from wooded banks which are
mindless of the log-jam   seething calmly off-shore.

Tanka

THEME: travelogue
FORM: 31 syllables
POEM LENGTH: 5 lines (5/7/5/7/7)
METRE: none
RHYME SCHEME: none
TENSE: generally present
TITLE: none

—   see HAIKU

BACKGROUND:
—   'tanka' (short poem)
—   definitive literary form in Japanese poetry (C7th)
—   generally written to mark occasion
—   Japanese imperial family still release tanka to celebrate new year

FORM:
—   unrhymed cinquain
—   similar to haiku but more syllables, & uses simile/metaphor/personification
—   able to contain two 'moments' rather than one (haiku)
—   *kami-no-ku* = upper phrase (5/7/5)
         shimo-no-ku = lower phrase (7/7)
—   3rd line often pivotal: reads one way with lines before, another way with lines following
—   line-break between 3rd & 4th lines acceptable/optional (not essential)
—   often composed as finale to moment/experience: no event complete without commemorated by tanka!
—   subjects include seasons/nature/travel/love/loss/other strong feelings
—   style is lyrical/elegant/musically expressive
—   tone is deeply emotional
—   must contain *suggestiveness beyond words* (indispensable feature)

TASK:
—   write three tanka, each encapsulating a moment (or two) while travelling
—   three tanka may or may not be related
—   landscape need not be Australian
—   consider tanka as visual snapshot underlined by deep emotion

READING:
—   Katherine Gallagher 'Tanka for a Hero' *Carnival Edge*
—   Beverley George *The Pinging Hail*
—   Chris Mansell 'Modern Tanka' *www.poetrylibrary.edu.au*
—   *Manyoshu*
—   Geoff Page 'Braidwood Tanka' *www.poetrylibrary.edu.au*
—   Peter Porter "Talking Shop' Tanka' *www.poetrylibrary.edu.au*
—   Masaoka Shiki

Tanka for a Hero
—Katherine Gallagher

Brave Monsieur Pognon
with a quarter of a heart,
his blood running cold;
he eats for the inner man,
can't believe the state he's in.

It's always the same—
his struggle to the clinic
for a transfusion:
the doctors give him hard hope
and the nurses crisp their smiles.

He takes it on the chin,
belives life's today's tipple
as his heart gears up
a season of good whisky
and meshes a young man's fire.

In the Resistance
he marched into the front-line,
wore his cocky cap,
filleting secrets that lost,
sometimes won, the local wars.

When his friends visit,
they rarely talk old battles:
dare devil escapes —
the risks of that other time,
its *do-or-die* calendar.

Monsieur Pognon knows
he has carried his chances,
his blood so thin now,
and he is left hard-memoried . . .
encircling his life, this death.

—Beverley George

slicing a lemon
with my sharpest knife
seeds remain in place
segments hold their structure
despite my child's divorce

Three Portraits of the Poet

THEME:	a known poet/an imaginary poet/yourself
FORM:	3 sestets
RHYME SCHEME:	none
METRE:	none
LINE LENGTH:	consistent

—   see SEQUENCE POEM

FORM:

—   select three related perspectives, one for each stanza, for example:

past, present, future

front view, profile, back view (photographs/mirror)

before, during, after

noon, sunset, 3am

1960, 1988, 2007

—   each 6-line stanza to be numerically identified

I. / II. / III.

i / ii / iii

1. / 2. / 3.

one / two / three

—   each stanza to end with a (different) tripartite line:

"It is dark. It is light. It is golden."

"she stops   stares   walks on"

"This is everywhere, this is nowhere: this is where he is."

"Alright. Okay. Just breathe . . ."

"Goodbye, goodbye. Goodbye."

—   rhythmic/emotive power of tripartite anchor:

"ready, set, GO!"

"veni, vidi, vici"

"left/right/left"

"Going, going, gone."

"For thine is the kingdom, the power & the glory . . ."

"Once. Twice. SOLD!"

TASK:

—   write an auto/biographical portrait in three sections

—   be as dispassionate as possible: brave/accurate/non-judgemental

—   try to convey essence of poet via three differing angles

READING:

—   Peter Bakowski 'Sylvia Plath writing in her journal, 23 Fitzroy Road, London, February 1963' *Beneath our Armour*

—   Michael Dransfield 'Colonial Poet' *Penguin Anthology of Australian Poetry*

—   Ted Hughes 'The Thought-Fox' *Norton Anthology of Poetry*

—   Geoffrey Lehmann 'Self Portrait at 62' *Australian Poetry Since 1788*

—   James McAuley 'Self-portrait, Newcastle 1942' *Penguin Anthology of Australian Poetry*

—   W.S. Merwin 'Berryman' *Selected Poems*

—   Geoff Page 'Pecking at the Glass' *Agnostic Skies*

—   Dylan Thomas 'In My Craft or Sullen Art' *Norton Anthology of Poetry*

Colonial Poet
—Michael Dransfield

today he will write some verses. his schedule
allows for a poem on his travels, or
                    roses, or
                    a mythological topic.
the day is hot so he selects the past / waterfalls,
dryads, a god or two. from the filing cabinet
of his head, in which legends are filed, alphabetically,
he picks out Hylas and a springside of nymphs. these tiny
      people
come to life for him, obediently; the ingredients mix well—
the beautiful youth / himself / the women / his / who take him
for their own. he makes of this an allegory, displaying his
      knowledge / minimal /
of psychology / referring to another file / and from the news,
a topical allusion. his measured cadences unfold, a page or two
      is covered;
he pauses, reviewing what is written. for him the parentheses
      ripple outward
pleasingly, and he sees in the still pool of his verse
a clear reflection of himself as god.
he rises, leaving the study, it has served its panelled purpose;
      switches off
his music machine. the record, labelled in flawless french
L'Apres-midi etc / returns to yet another file, and his gods and
little people
go home to their woods
as far now from his mind
as the toy soldiers of his childhood

Berryman
—W.S. Merwin

I will tell you what he told me
in the years just after the war
as we then called
the second world war

don't lose your arrogance yet he said
you can do that when you're older
lose it too soon and you may
merely replace it with vanity

just one time he suggested
changing the usual order
of the same words in a line of verse
why point out a thing twice

he suggested I pray to the Muse
get down on my knees and pray
right there in the corner
and he said he meant it literally

it was in the days before the beard
and the drink but he was deep
in tides of his own through which he sailed
chin sideways and head tilted like a tacking sloop

he was far older than the dates allowed for
much older than I was he was in his thirties
he snapped down his nose with an accent
I think he had affected in England

as for publishing he advised me
to paper my wall with rejection slips
his lips and the bones of his long fingers trembled
with the vehemence of his views about poetry

he said the great presence
that permitted everything and transmuted it
in poetry was passion
passion was genius and he praised movement and invention

I had hardly begun to read
I asked how can you ever be sure
that what you write is really
any good at all and he said you can't

you can't you can never be sure
you die without knowing
whether anything you wrote was any good
if you have to be sure don't write

Self-portrait, Newcastle 1942
—James McAuley

First day, by the open window,
He sits at a table to write,
And watches the coal-dust settle
Black on the paper's white.

Years of breathing this grime
Show black in the lungs of the dead
When autopsies are done;
So at least it is said.

Sunset over the steelworks
Bleeds a long rubric of war;
He thinks he knows, but doesn't,
The black print of the score.

He, like that sullied paper,
Has acquired no meaning yet.
He goes for long walks at night,
Or drinks with people he's met.

In sleeping panic he shatters
The glass of a window-pane.
What will he do with his life?
Jump three storeys down in the rain?

Something—guilt, tension, or outrage—
Keeps coming in nightmare shape.
Screams often startle the house:
He leaps up blind to escape.

By day he teaches the dullest
Intermediate class;
He gets on well with them, knowing
He too has a test to pass.

With friends he talks anarchism,
The philosophical kind,
But *Briefe an einen jungen
Dichter* speaks close to his mind.

Tree Poem

THEME:	a single tree of personal/historical/mythological significance
FORM:	block
RHYME SCHEME:	a/b/c (internal)
METRE:	none
POEM LENGTH:	maximum 20 lines
TENSE:	present

FORM:

—   select three main sounds ('a', 'b', 'c')

—   utilise each sound at least six times throughout body of poem

—   avoid end-of-line rhyming

—   utilise (common) tree name in title

TASK:

—   choose one specific tree as main character/hero of poem

—   research botanical characteristics of tree

—   imbue tree with emotional import

—   gradually reveal emotional import via description & metaphor

—   slowly disclose significance of tree's 'message' to you

READING:

—   Judith Beveridge 'Ficus Religiosa' *Wolf Notes*

—   Jack Davis 'Death of a Tree' *Penguin Anthology of Australian Poetry*

—   Mary Gilmore 'The Yarran-tree' *P&W Anthology of Australian Poetry*

—   John Shaw Nielson 'The Orange Tree' *P&W Anthology of Australian Poetry*

—   Oodgeroo Noonuccal 'Municipal Gum' *Penguin Anthology of Australian Poetry*

—   Mark O'Connor 'The Olive Tree' *Australian Poetry Since 1788*

—   Mary Oliver 'The Black Walnut Tree' *www.writersalmanac.publicradio.org*

—   Michael Pembroke *Trees of History & Romance*

—   Sylvia Plath 'The Moon and the Yew Tree' *Ariel*

—   Petra White 'Karri Forest' *A Hunger*

The Yarran-tree
—Mary Gilmore

The Lady of the Yarran-tree,
        She built herself a house,
And, happy in it, there she lived
        As tidy as a mouse;
She set a stool against the fire,
        And hung the broom beside,
And yet, although she sat alone,
        The door was open wide.

And she beside the Yarran-tree
        Was busy as could be;
She kept her sheep, she carded wool,
        Her bleach was white to see;
She baked her bread from wheat she grew,
        She tanned the good ox-hide;
And still, for all she sat alone,
        Her door was open wide.

The Lady of the Yarran-tree
        Looked out, one night, and saw
The dark hand of a stranger reach
        To lay on her his law;
She rose and drew the curtain close,
        Her little lamp to hide—
And yet, for all she was alone,
        The door stood open wide.

I asked her if she didn't know
        The fears of woman-kind,
That, though by day they come and go,
        Are still within the mind.
She looked at me and slowly said,
        'Such fears in me abide!'
And yet I knew she sat alone,
        The door left open wide.

The Yarran-tree against the spring
        Put on its amber green,
Like golden berries, on each twig,
        Its blossoms all were seen;
I saw the stranger watch the tree,
        The woman there inside—
And still, although she sat alone,
        The door was open wide.

To her beside the Yarran-tree,
        I said, 'Go buy a ring,
A ring of silver laced with steel,
        From which a shot may sing

Then, when the stranger hears the song,
        As winds shall bear it wide,
It will be safe to sit alone,
        The house-door open wide.'

Then she beside the Yarran-tree,
        She turned and looked at me,
She laid the spinning from her hand,
        And spake as still could be;
'Go you,' she said, 'and make the ring,
        And make of it your pride;
That I may safely sit alone,
        The door set open wide.'

I took the woman at her word,
        And straitly there I made
A ring of silver laced with steel,
        That sang as trumpets played;
I set it down against the step,
        And, though the door is wide,
The Lady of the Yarran-tree
        Dwells ever safe inside.

The Orange Tree
—John Shaw Neilson

The young girl stood beside me. I
          Saw not what her young eyes could see:
—A light, she said, not of the sky
          Lives somewhere in the Orange Tree.

—Is it, I said, of east or west?
          The heartbeat of a luminous boy
Who with his faltering flute confessed
          Only the edges of his joy?

Was he, I said, borne to the blue
          In a mad escapade of Spring
Ere he could make a fond adieu
          To his love in the blossoming?

—Listen! the young girl said. There calls
          No voice, no music beats on me;
But it is almost sound: it falls
          This evening on the Orange Tree.

—Does he, I said, so fear the Spring
          Ere the white sap too far can climb?
See in the full gold evening
          All happenings of the olden time?

Is he so goaded by the green?
          Does the compulsion of the dew
Make him unknowable but keen
          Asking with beauty of the blue?

—Listen! the young girl said. For all
          Your hapless talk you fail to see
There is a light, a step, a call
          This evening on the Orange Tree.

—Is it, I said, a waste of love
          Imperishably old in pain,
Moving as an affrighted dove
          Under the sunlight or the rain?

Is it a fluttering heart that gave
          Too willingly and was reviled?
Is it the stammering at a grave,
          The last word of a little child?

—Silence! the young girl said. Oh, why,
          Why will you talk to weary me?
Plague me no longer now, for I
          Am listening like the Orange Tree.

The Olive Tree
—Mark O'Connor

Nobody knows how long it takes to kill an olive.
Drought, axe, fire, are admitted failures. Hack one down,
grub out a ton of mainroot for fuel, and next spring
every side-root sends up shoots. A great frost
can leave the trees leafless for years; they revive.
Invading armies will fell them. They return
through the burnt-out ribs of siege machines.

Only the patient goat, nibbling his way down the ages,
has malice to master the olive. Sometimes, they say,
a man finds a dead orchard, fired and goat-
cropped centuries back. He settles and fences;
the stumps revive. His grandchildren's family prosper
by the arduous oil-pressing trade. Then wars
and disease wash over. Goats return. The olives
go under, waiting another age.

Their shade still lies where Socrates disputed.
Gethsemane's withered groves are bearing yet.

Karri Forest
—Petra White

near Manjimup, Western Australia

It swirls you in its poem, slows the protester
chained to a tree, the logger chainsawing his
future together, to the pace of chessmen,
in a battle that must be waged one-tree-at-
a-time on moral ground stodgy as mud.

Sepia tangles of tree-waste, the earth
lifting its bare prickly head: what to do
with all this light—is it light? At night I walked
into the forest (what remained). Moonlight
brazened on the scabby wood, red Xs

scrawled on bark; already there, the dead tree
across my path I couldn't seem to cross,
the corpse I killed and buried and forgot,
in a dream that wakes and circles, always
convinces, as one's guilt always feels right.

Villanelle

THEME: longing
FORM: 5 tercets & final quatrain (with repeated lines)
POEM LENGTH: 19 lines
METRE: none (note Dylan Thomas has added decasyllabic construction...)
RHYME SCHEME: aba//abaa

—   see MONOCHORD, SYLLABIC POEM

BACKGROUND:
—   'villanelle' from Italian *villano* (peasant)/Latin *villa* (country house/farm)
—   a round originally sung to repetitive agrarian tasks (scything/sheaf binding)
—   canonical villanelle operational from C16th (France > Jean Passerat)
—   popular in English C20th

FORM:
—   form based on set line repetitions:
         1st line of 1st stanza repeated as last line of 2nd & 4th stanzas
         3rd line of 1st stanza repeated as last line of 3rd & 5th stanzas
         these two refrains repeated as penultimate & ultimate lines
—   1, 2, 3 / 4, 5, 6(1) / 7, 8, 9(3) / 10, 11, 12(1) / 13, 14, 15(3) / 16, 17, 18(1), 19(3)
—   aba(a) rhyme scheme constructed according to refrains
—   absence of narrative possibility > reluctant to tell 'story'
—   circles around, suggesting recurrences of mood/emotion/memory
—   formal properties directly address concept of loss
—   refuses forward motion: embraces temporality, & finally dissolution
—   each stanza, with refrains, becomes a series of retrievals

TASK:
—   construct a minimum of 13 monochords
—   7 'a' rhymes ("ing")
—   6 'b' rhymes ("all" / "le")
—   class villanelle: two monochords per student
—   individual villanelle: any two rhymes

READING:
—   W.H. Auden 'If I Could Tell You' *Collected Poems*
—   Connie Barber 'Of the Nature of Lemons' *The Road South*
—   Elizabeth Bishop 'One Art' *The Complete Poems*
—   Dan Disney 'nothing mystical, it's like 'hey have an aspirin'' *Mannequin's Guide to Utopias*
—   Francesca Haig 'Villanelle for a pregnancy test' *Motherlode*
—   Mal McKimmie 'Villanelle to the muse from a disgruntled poet' *Poetileptic*
—   James Merrill 'The World and the Child' *Collected Poems*
—   Dylan Thomas 'Do not go gentle into that good night' *Seven Centuries*

nothing mystical, it's like 'hey have an aspirin'
—Dan Disney

nothing mystical, it's like 'hey have an aspirin'
        the crazy breeders uttering injunctions like painted blue jays.
                When they get to town nobody sleeps until they're gone

willy-nilly as divine accidents amid the particularity of things.
        Inert as an absurdly large rule, they are
                nothing mystical, like 'hey have a complex insecurity'

categorical with basic speech, this awkward climate
        of hierarchies confused with delight.
                When they get to town nobody sleeps until they're gone

and nobody enters the *yes-no* dualism of *I-don't-know* ... underfoot
        the ground trickles with cats, trees, history
                it's nothing mystical, it's like 'hey have a programmatic soul'

they're smiling back like bad paintings or a hands-on cure
        rehearsing with ginger ale.
                When they get to town nobody sleeps until they're gone

casual as cut moonlight
        and lonely as a surgical experience, pleasantly moist;
                nothing mystical, it's like 'hey have an aspirin'
                when they get to town nobody sleeps until they're gone

Warm-Up Exercises (supplement)

LINE TURN EXERCISES

Poem
—William Carlos Williams (*Seven Centuries*)

As the cat
climbed over
the top of

the jamcloset
first the right
forefoot

carefully
then the hind
stepped down

into the pit of
the empty
flowerpot

53
—e e cummings (*73 poems*)

of all things under our
blonder than blondest star

the most mysterious
(eliena, my dear) is this

—how anyone so gay
possibly could die

EYE RHYME EXERCISE

1	"oo"	through
2	"uff"	tough
3	"oh"	although
4	"ow"	bough
5	"a"	Scarborough
6	"or"	ought
7	"off"	trough
8	"up"	hiccough

Glossary

accent	natural falling of a beat within a poetic foot > also, *stress*
alliteration	consonants—usually initial—repeated in succession
	example: a lovely little clutch of clams
anacrusis	weak syllable (or off-beat) at beginning of line
anaphora	word/phrase repeated at beginning of successive clauses
anapaest	ternary (or triple) poetic foot, with accent on third syllable
	examples: interrupt; reconnect; move away
assonance	vowel sounds—usually internal—repeated in succession
	example: don't go far from home alone
binary	poetic foot consisting of two syllables > also, *duple*
	examples: iamb; pyrrhic; spondee; trochee
burden	line or phrase repeated through poem, usually at end of stanza > also, *refrain*
caesura	pause (or breath) within a line
catachresis	mixed metaphor
	examples: a rolling stone gathers no wool; a watched clock never boils
chiasmus	figure repeated in reverse > either content or form
	examples: worth/evil/ill/virtue; abba; abccba; abcdcba
cliché	well-known phrase, repeated verbatim
colloquy	conversation
concatenation	series of linked items/events
conceit	elaborate metaphor
couplet	two lines of poetry, often rhymed
dactyl	ternary (or triple) poetic foot, with accent on first syllable
	examples: poetry; Saturday; answer it
dénouement	natural resolution of poem, usually occurring close to or at end
diphthong	syllable where sound moves from one vowel sound to another > may be counted as one *or* two syllables in syllabic verse
	examples: cloud; lion; year
elision	omission of word, or part of word, often due to contraction
	examples: you're; leavin'; gonna
enjambment	when end of sentence or phrase does not coincide with end of line
envoi	short concluding stanza, similar to coda in music or epilogue in prose
heptameter	line comprising seven poetic feet
hexameter	line comprising six poetic feet
iamb	binary (or duple) poetic foot, with accent on second syllable
	examples: remote; decide; the cold
lacuna	visual space or gap within line, often used in place of punctuation
metaphor	figure of speech whereby one thing is described in terms of another > also, *trope*
	examples: eyes glued to the tv; keep it under your hat
metre	measured rhythm based on regularly recurring accentual patterns
mimesis	imitation, usually of true life
monochord	one line of poetry
octave	stanza comprising eight lines
oxymoron	figure of speech comprising apparently contradictory terms
	example: the silence is deafening
parody	imitation which exaggerates or ridicules original > also, *satire*
pentameter	line comprising five poetic feet
poetic foot	metrical unit which creates rhythm when used as regularly repeating pattern
prosody	patterns of rhythm and sound

pyrrhic	binary (or duple) poetic foot comprising two short unstressed syllables, usually small functional utilities examples: it is; when the; if you
quatrain	stanza comprising four lines
quintain	stanza comprising five lines > also, *cinquain*
repetend	word or phrase repeated through poem, often at end of line
rhyme	corresponding sounds (or visual appearance) of words
rhythm	recognisable beat or pulse
scansion	method of scanning (analysing) poetry to determine metre/rhythm
septet	stanza comprising seven lines
sestet	stanza comprising six lines
simile	figure of speech whereby one thing is compared to another, often involving words "as" or "like" examples: working like a dog; as good as gold
soliloquy	thoughts spoken aloud by one person
spondee	binary (or duple) poetic foot comprising two short stressed syllables examples: north-west; outside; the end
stanza	group of lines in poetry, with number of lines regularly repeated in other verses
syllable	word or part of word containing vowel, functioning as unit of sound/pronunciation

synecdoche	figure of speech whereby a whole is *reduced* to one of its parts, or a whole *represents* one of its parts
	    examples: she parked her wheels [car] outside;
	    he called [one or two of] the Police

teleuton	last word of line > also, *end-word*
tercet	stanza comprising three lines
tetrameter	line comprising four poetic feet
trimeter	line comprising three poetic feet
trochee	binary (or duple) poetic foot, with accent on first syllable examples: <u>Tues</u>day; <u>fa</u>ther; <u>bought</u> it
verse	group of lines in poetry, not necessarily same length as other verses in poem
virgule	forward slash, sometimes used in place of punctuation in modern poems
volta	where initial mood or thought undergoes change, often preceded by space between lines or stanzas, rarely occurring more than once in a poem > also, *turn*

Bibliography

Anthologies

— Aitken, Adam, Kim Cheng Boey & Michelle Cahill, eds. *Contemporary Asian Australian Poets*. Sydney: Puncher, 2013.

— Allison, Alexander W., et al., eds. *Norton Anthology of Poetry*. 3rd ed. New York: Norton, 1983.

— Harrison, Jennifer & Kate Waterhouse, eds. *Motherlode: Australian Women's Poetry 1986–2008*. Sydney: Puncher, 2009.

— Jose, Nicholas, et al., eds. *Macquarie PEN Anthology of Australian Literature*. Sydney: Allen, 2009.

— Kelen, Kit, ed. *Notes for the Translators from 142 New Zealand and Australian Poets*. Macao: ASM, 2013.

— Kinsella, John, ed. *Penguin Anthology of Australian Poetry*. Melbourne: Penguin, 2009.

— Kinsella, John, ed. *Turnrow Anthology of Contemporary Australian Poetry*. Louisiana: Turnrow: 2014.

— Leonard, John, ed. *New Music: An Anthology of Contemporary Australian Poetry*. Wollongong: Five Islands, 2001.

— Leonard, John, ed. *Puncher & Wattmann Anthology of Australian Poetry*. Sydney: Puncher, 2009.

— Leonard, John, ed. *Seven Centuries of Poetry in English*. 5th ed. Melbourne: Oxford, 2003.

— Page, Geoff, ed. *Indigo Book of Modern Australian Sonnets*. Canberra: Ginninderra, 2003.

— Pretty, Ron, ed. *The Road South: An Anthology of Contemporary Australian Poetry*. Kolkota: Bengal, 2007.

— Schmidt, Elizabeth Hun, ed. *Poets Laureate Anthology*. New York: Norton, 2010.

— Strand, Mark, ed. *100 Great Poems of the Twentieth Century*. New York: Norton, 2005.

— Strauss, Jennifer, ed. *Family Ties: Australian Poems of the Family*. Melbourne: Oxford, 1998.

— Tredinnick, Mark, ed. *Australian Love Poems*. 2nd ed. Melbourne: Inkerman, 2014.

Individual Titles

— Adamson, Robert. *The Golden Bird: New & Selected Poems*. Melbourne: Black Inc., 2008.

— Albiston, Jordie. *Botany Bay Document: A Poetic History of the Women of Botany Bay*. 3rd ed. Melbourne: Black Pepper, 2013.

— ---. *the sonnet according to 'm'*. Melbourne: Leonard, 2009.

— Anderson, John. *The Shadow's Keep*. Melbourne: Black Pepper, 1997.

— Apollinaire, Guillaume. *Calligrammes*. Paris: Gallimard, 1995.

— Ashbery, John. *Planisphere: New Poems*. New York: Ecco, 2010.

— Atwood, Margaret. *The Journals of Susanna Moodie*. Boston: Houghton, 1997.

— Auden, W.H. *Collected Poems*. Ed. Edward Mendelson. London: Faber, 1994.

— Bakowski, Peter. *Beneath our Armour*. Melbourne: Hunter, 2009.

— Ballou, Emily. *The Darwin Poems*. Perth: U of Western Australia P, 2009.

— Beaver, Bruce. *The Long Game*. Brisbane: U of Queensland P, 2005.

— Beveridge, Judith. *Storm and Honey*. Sydney: Giramondo, 2009.

— ---. *Wolf Notes*. Sydney: Giramondo, 2003.

— Bishop, Elizabeth. *The Complete Poems 1927-1979*. New York: Farrar, 1983.

— Boyle, Peter. *Towns in the Great Desert: New & Selected Poems*. Sydney: Puncher, 2013.

— Cahill, Michelle. *Vishvarupa*. Melbourne: Five Islands, 2011.

— Caldwell, Grant. *glass clouds*. Melbourne: Five Islands, 2010.

— Campbell, Elizabeth. *Error*. Melbourne: Leonard, 2011.

— Carroll, Lewis. *The Annotated Alice*. Ed. Martin Gardner. London: Penguin, 1970.

— Carson, Anne M. *Removing the Kimono*. Melbourne: Hybrid, 2013.

— Clarke, John. *The Even More Complete Book of Australian Verse*. Melbourne: Text, 2003.

— Cohen, Leonard. *The Concise Leonard Cohen*. London: Wise, 1997.

— cummings, e e. *73 poems*. New York: Liveright, 2003.

— Davidson, Toby. *Beast Language*. Melbourne: Five Islands, 2012.

— Dawe, Bruce. *Sometimes Gladness: Collected Poems 1954–1997*. 5th ed. Melbourne: Longman, 2002.

— Day, Sarah. *Grass Notes*. Blackheath: Brandl, 2009.

— Disney, Dan. *and then when the*. Melbourne: Leonard, 2011.

— ---. *Mannequin's Guide to Utopias*. Macao: Flying Island, 2014.

— Edgar, Stephen. *Other Summers*. Melbourne: Black Pepper, 2006.

— Emery, Brook. *Collusion*. Melbourne: Leonard, 2012.

— Fitch, Toby. *Rawshock*. Sydney: Puncher, 2012.

— Forbes, John. *Collected Poems*. Sydney: Brandl, 2001.

— Ford, Lorin. *a wattle seedpod*. Brisbane: Post Pressed, 2008.

— Gallagher, Katherine. *Carnival Edge: New & Selected Poems*. Todmorden: Arc, 2010.

— Fry, Stephen. *The Ode Less Travelled: Unlocking the Poet Within*. London: Arrow, 2007.

— Gaskin, Claire. *a bud*. Melbourne: Leonard, 2006.

— ---. *Paperweight*. Melbourne: Hunter, 2013.

— George, Beverley. *The Birds That Stay*. Sydney: Eucalypt, 2013.

— ---. *This Pinging Hail*. Sydney: Eucalypt, 2012.

— Ginsberg, Allen. *Howl, Kaddish and Other Poems*. New York: Penguin, 2010.

— Gould, Alan. *The Past Completes Me: Selected Poems 1973–2003*. Brisbane: U of Queensland P, 2005.

— Gray, Robert. *Coast Road: Selected Poems*. Melbourne: Black Inc., 2014.

— Hart, Libby. *This Floating World*. Melbourne: Five Islands, 2011.

— Harwood, Gwen. *Bone Scan*. Sydney: Angus, 1998.

— ---. *Mappings of the Plane: New Selected Poems*. Eds. Gregory Kratzmann & Chris Wallace-Crabbe. Manchester: Fyfield, 2009.

— Hawthorne, Susan. *Earth's Breath*. Melbourne: Spinifex, 2009.

— Hemensley, Kris. *My Life In Theatre*. Sydney: River Road, 2009. cd.

— Hetherington, Matt. *sweeping the dust: indian haiku & senryu*. Melbourne: Precious, 2005.

— Hetherington, Paul. *Six Different Windows*. Perth: U of Western Australia P, 2013.

— Hollander, John. *Rhyme's Reason: A Guide to English Verse*. 3rd ed. New Haven: Yale UP, 2001.

— Holt, L.K. *Keeps*. Melbourne: Leonard, 2014.

— ---. *Man Wolf Man*. Melbourne: Leonard, 2007.

— Jenkins, John. *Growing up with Mr Menzies*. Melbourne: Leonard, 2008.

— Johnson, Judy. *Nomadic*. Melbourne: Black Pepper, 2004.

— Keats, John. *John Keats: The Complete Poems*. Ed. John Barnard. 3rd ed. London: Penguin, 1988.

— Kelly, David. *Book*. Melbourne: Eaglemont, 2000.

— Kissane, Andy. *Out to Lunch*. Sydney: Puncher, 2009.

— Kooser, Ted. *The Blizzard Voices*. 2nd ed. Lincoln: U of Nebraska P, 2006.

— Lawrence, Anthony. *New and Selected Poems*. Brisbane: U of Queensland P, 1998.

— ---. *Signal Flare*. Sydney: Puncher, 2013.

— Lehman, David. *The Daily Mirror: A Journal in Poetry*. New York: Scribner, 2000.

— McBryde, Ian. *Equatorial*. Wollongong: Five Islands, 2001.

— ---. *Flank*. Melbourne: Eaglemont, 1998.

— ---. *Slivers*. Melbourne: Flat Chat, 2005.

— McKimmie, Mal. *Poetileptic*. Melbourne: Five Islands, 2005.

— Martel, Yann. *Beatrice and Virgil*. Toronto: Random, 2010.

— Mateer, John. *Barefoot Speech*. Fremantle: Fremantle Arts Centre, 2000.

— Merrill, James. *Collected Poems*. New York: Knopf, 2001.

— Merwin, W.S. *Selected Poems*. Northumberland: Bloodaxe, 2007.

— Middleton, Kate. *Ephemeral Waters*. Sydney: Giramondo, 2013.

— ---. *Fire Season*. Sydney: Giramondo, 2009.

— Murray, Les. *Collected Poems*. Melbourne: Black Inc., 2006.

— Musgrave, David. *Phantom Limb*. Melbourne: Leonard, 2010.

— Oliver, Mary. *A Poetry Handbook*. Orlando: Harcourt, 1994.

— Ondaatje, Michael. *The Collected Works of Billy the Kid*. New York: Vintage, 1996.

— Owen, Jan. *Poems 1980–2008*. Melbourne: Leonard, 2008.

— Page, Geoff. *Agnostic Skies*. Melbourne: Five Islands, 2006.

— Pembroke, Michael. *Trees of History & Romance*. Melbourne: Bloomings, 2009.

— Petrarch, Francesco. *The Poetry of Petrarch*. Trans. David Young. New York: Farrar, 2004.

— Plath, Sylvia. *Ariel*. New York: Harper, 2001.

— Pretty, Ron. *what the afternoon knows*. Sydney: Pitt Street, 2013.

— Rich, Adrienne. *The Fact of a Doorframe*. New York: Norton, 2002.

— Ritsos, Yannis. *Monochords*. Sydney: Paper Bark, 1996.

— Rossetti, Christina. *Goblin Market: a tale of two sisters*. San Francisco: Chronicle, 1997.

— Ryan, Gig. *New and Selected Poems*. Sydney: Giramondo, 2011.

— Salom, Philip. *New and Selected Poems*. Fremantle: Fremantle Arts Centre, 1998.

— Shapcott, Tom. *Shabbytown Calendar*. 2nd ed. Brisbane: U of Queensland P, 1987.

— Sharkey, Michael. *Another Fine Morning in Paradise*. Melbourne: Five Islands, 2012.

— Shonagon, Sei. *The Pillow Book*. Trans. Meredith McKinney. London: Penguin, 2007.

— Simic, Charles. *The World Doesn't End*. New York: Harcourt, 1985.

— Skovron, Alex. *Autographs*. Melbourne: Hybrid, 2008.

— ---. *Infinite City: 100 Sonnetinas*. Wollongong: Five Islands, 1999.

— ---. *Sleeve Notes*. Sydney: Hale, 1992.

— ---. *Towards the Equator: New & Selected Poems*. Sydney: Puncher, 2014.

— Starbuck, George. *The Works*. Eds. Kathryn Starbuck & Elizabeth Meese. Tuscaloosa: U of Alabama P, 2003.

— Sykes, Patricia. *Wire Dancing*. Melbourne: Spinifex, 1999.

— Watson, John. *A First Reader*. Wollongong: Five Islands, 2003.

— White, Petra. *A Hunger*. Melbourne: Leonard, 2014.

— Wilkinson, Jessica L. *marionette: a biography of miss marion davies*. Sydney: Vagabond, 2012.

— Williams, W.C. *Paterson*. Ed. Christopher MacGowan. New York: New Directions, 1995.

— Wordsworth, William. *The Works of William Wordsworth*. Hertfordshire: Wordsworth, 1994.

— Wright, Judith. *Phantom Dwelling*. London: Virago, 1986.

Websites

— *bhtafe.edu.au/divan*

— *bobdylan.com*

— *chesterton.org*

— *cranberrydesigns.com*

— *foundpoetryreview.com*

— *poemhunter.com*

— *poetryfoundation.org*

— *poetrylibrary.edu.au*

— *slate.com*

— *verbatimpoetry.blogspot.com*

— *writersalmanac.publicradio.org*

Every effort has been made to obtain permission for the use of copyright material reproduced in this book, but in some cases copyright holders could not be traced. We welcome any information in this regard. An additional list acknowledging original sources can be found at http://www.puncherandwattmann.com/books/book/the-weekly-poem/ .

www.ingramcontent.com/pod-product-compliance
Lightning Source LLC
Chambersburg PA
CBHW080858090426

42737CB00015B/2984